AF445721

Devotions Of a Layman

Book One

By: Lee Carson

PROISLE PUBLISHING
SERVICES LLC

John 3:16-18

¹⁶ For God so loved the world that he gave his one and only Son, that whoever believes in him shall not perish but have eternal life. ¹⁷ For God did not send his Son into the world to condemn the world, but to save the world through him. ¹⁸ Whoever believes in him is not condemned, but whoever does not believe stands condemned already because they have not believed in the name of God's one and only Son.

These thoughts are a collection of memories. Memories of things I have heard and experiences of days I've lived over the past eighty-four years and are dedicated to my friends and extended family of the

First United Methodist Church Bullard, Texas

Scripture Quotes Are From

The New King James Version (NKJV)
And
The Common English Bible (CEB)

The contents of this work, including, but not limited to, the accuracy of events, people, and places depicted; opinions expressed; permission to used previously published materials included; and any advice given or actions advocated are solely the responsibility of the author, who assumes all liability for said work and indemnifies the publisher against any claims stemming from publication of the work.

All Rights Reserved

Copyright © 2019 by Lee Carson

No part of this book may be reproduced or transmitted in any form or by any means, electronic or mechanical, including photocopying, recording, or by any information storage and retrieval system, without permission in writing from the copyright owner. The views expressed in this work are solely those of the author and do not necessarily reflect the views of the publisher, and the publisher disclaims any responsibility for them. Any people depicted in stock imagery provided by Getty Images are models, such images are being used for illustrative purposes only.

Proisle Publishing Services LLC
1177 6th Ave 5th Floor
New York, NY 10036, USA
Phone: (+1 347-922-3779)
info@proislepublishing.com

ISBN: 979-8-9855817-5-1

The Gospel in Short

When Jesus started his ministry, those who followed him were the common people. They listened to his words, even though he too was a common man. As the son of a carpenter he was trained to be a carpenter. He had no position, no credentials, and was never thought of as anyone who had authority, unless you believed what was said about a voice from the sky, as reported in Matthew 3:17, *"And a voice from heaven said, "This is my Son, whom I love; with him I am well pleased."*

Jesus had no religious, scholarly, or political position, yet the common people thought what he had to say was authoritative, contained wisdom, power, and knowledge. They didn't see this in their leaders, who saw Jesus as a man who was going to be a radical trouble maker. Matthew 7:28-29 says, *When Jesus had finished saying these things, the crowds were amazed at his teaching, because he taught as one who had authority, and not as their teachers of the law.*

The educated leaders were looking for His credentials. The common people were looking for reality. The crowds grew. Talk about him spread. It was beginning to look as if Jesus could become a threat to the intellectual community. The dominate leaders of Jesus day were the Pharisees and Sadducees and both groups began pressing Jesus with questions. First it was the Pharisees and then the Sadducees trying to catch him off guard and make him look foolish. Finally, he was asked, "What is the most important commandment?" In Luke 10:27 He answered, with a summary of the Ten Commandments. *"'Love the Lord your God with all your heart and with all your soul and with all your strength and with all your mind'; and, 'Love your neighbor as yourself.'"*

After three and a half years as an itinerate preacher, he died on a cross for the forgiveness of the world's sins, and on the third day rose from his grave. In Luke 24 He told us to go into the world teaching the gospel to everyone and then ascended to Heaven. Jesus is our savior, the son of God. He died for the sins of every person who believes this, and asks for forgiveness.

"Father, Abba, thank you for your son Jesus." AMEN

Amazing Grace

Christians use many words that sound churchy, secret, or special to non-Christians. They're good words, meaningful, and necessary, but not used in every day secular language. To the un-churched we must seem like a secret order. One such word is "grace." In the NIV it's found 131 times and plays a significant role in our faith. Grace, and variations of it have many meanings.

Grace can be a name. I had a great aunt named Grace. There was Grace Kelly, Gracie Allen, wife of George Burns, and my neighbor's little granddaughter Mary Grace. Grace is a good name.

Grace can mean beauty of form or movement, like a ballet dancer. It can be charm or elegance, and an agreeable quality in either feminine or manly grace.

Grace is a short prayer of thanks before a meal.
Extra time to pay debts or accomplish tasks is a grace period.

It is mercy, clemency, pardon, forgiveness and can mean good will, favor, kindness, love freely given, or a gift without debt.

In Christianity, grace is the term referring to God's freely given love, and His action of forgiving.

Christianity teaches that people need grace because they cannot overcome the effects of sin by themselves. People need God's grace for the forgiveness of sin, and we regard Jesus as the primary bearer of grace. Grace cannot be earned, only accepted as a free gift. Our response to God's grace is that of doing His work of teaching, healing, feeding and caring for others.

Ephesians 2:8-10 *"For it is by grace you have been saved, through faith—and this is not from yourselves, it is the gift of God— [9] not by works, so that no one can boast. [10] For we are God's handiwork, created in Christ Jesus to do good works, which God prepared in advance for us to do."* Isn't grace a good word?

"Thank you, God, for Your Grace, so freely given to us. AMEN"

Letters, Old and New

My wife and I met while I was in the army and were married just before I shipped out to Korea. When I gave the address for her to receive her allotment I ran into trouble. It couldn't be sent to her at Crystal Spring, Pa. There had to be a complete address. I explained that the post office was a small building in front of the general store, there was only the postmaster and one mailman with one route and they knew everyone. That didn't matter. There had to be a street or box number before it could be processed. I had to think of something, and knowing that if I could get it to Crystal Spring there would be no problem. So, I gave the address as Route 1, box 1, Crystal Spring, Pa. and that made everyone happy. Today everyone on that route has a box number and the post office, which has been moved inside the general store, has a zip code.

In the Old Testament, there can be found references to letters written to and from Kings and others on several various subjects. In the new testament, there are several letters that make some of our New Testament books, including the letters from Paul concerning various subjects. Here are some examples.

Ezra 4:11 "(This is a copy of the letter they sent him.) To King Artaxerxes, From your servants in Trans-Euphrates:"

I Corinthians 5:9 "I wrote to you in my letter not to associate with sexually immoral people– "

II Thessalonians 2:15 "So then, brothers and sisters, stand firm and hold fast to the teachings we passed on to you, whether by word of mouth or by letter."

Isn't it great that God's technology is different than ours? No glitches, no crashes, always the same, yesterday, today and tomorrow, and his address is always the same as we pray:

"Our Father Who Art in Heaven," we thank you that you are always the same, that you always receive our messages, and respond to them. AMEN"

Respectability

Opinions of people with power and authority, skilled at a craft, or at management, are sought out because they are respected. Everyone likes to be greeted with a smile and treated with respect. No matter who you are it is just down right nice to be respected. Respect seems such a small word yet everyone wants it. But, how do you show respect to others if they are unrespectable or when they show no respect toward you?

Sam always had something good to say about every person he met. He had little eulogies for everyone who died and was always able to say nice things about even the worst sinners. In the same town was a drunk who worked only long enough to meet his own needs and buy another bottle. His wife, with a little help from the good town folk, supported herself and their children. One cold winter morning the drunk was found in an alley where he had passed out and froze to death. The whole town turned out for the funeral just to hear what good thing Sam could possibly say. As he left the church Sam said," He was the best whistler I ever heard."

Luke 6:28 says, "Bless those who curse you, pray for those who mistreat you. 29 If someone strikes you on one cheek, turn to him the other also. If someone takes your cloak, do not stop him from taking your tunic. 30 Give to everyone who asks you, and if anyone takes what belongs to you, do not demand it back. 31 Do to others as you would have them do to you.

At times, it is difficult to leave the judging up to God. We want to say, "God if you only knew him like I do you would understand." But that isn't God's way and He doesn't mean for it to be ours. Often I fail, but there is always the opportunity to apologize and start over, and if for no other reason, showing respect for others sure helps you sleep.

"Father, hear us as we pray, that we might show respect to all with whom we have contact. AMEN"

A Growing Faith

It is dry, very dry. This is our second year of having a shortfall of rain. But, it will rain. I can't tell you when, but it will.

Black Sunday occurred on Easter Sunday 1935. The Midwest, the heartland of America, was parched. It hadn't rained in many months. Dust storms were getting more and more common. On Black Sunday, a gigantic windstorm developed just east of the Rockies. The winds blew at high speeds, picking up dirt from the dry, bare, prairie land. A dust cloud six miles high swept across Kansas, Nebraska, on and on across the Mississippi valley. When it was over, topsoil from dry fields lay deep over homes, barns, and anything in its way. The rain finally came and the weather returned to normal. Stories of "The Dust Bowl" of the 30's inspired the book and movie, "Grapes of Wrath."

A drought was threatening the crops around a small town and on a hot, dry, Sunday, a pastor told his congregation, "Faith is all that will save us. Everyone go home! Pray!" They did as they were told and returned to church the following Sunday. As soon as the pastor saw them he said, "We can't worship without faith. Where are your umbrellas?"

Matthew 17:20 *"Because you have so little faith. I tell you the truth, if you have faith as small as a mustard seed, you can say to this mountain, 'Move from here to there' and it will move. Nothing will be impossible for you."*

The author of Hebrews spends the entire eleventh chapter speaking of faith. *11:1 "Now faith is being sure of what we hope for and certain of what we do not see."*

I am afraid that I am so much like Peter. My faith would be strong enough to walk on water only if I were holding the Master's hand. By myself I am too weak. I would drown.

William Hinson, former pastor of Houston's FUMC said, "Life is a mystery. Faith helps us withstand more than it helps us understand."

Prayer without faith is just so many words. I have a way to go, but I am working on it. How is your trip going?

"Lord, help us to practice, practice, practice our faith, giving us the faith to believe and be strong for you. AMEN"

Growing as a Christian

I marvel at athletes, musicians, actors and others who do so well the things that most of us only dream of doing. Last week we attended a concert of "The Rhythm Brothers." All four of them are certainly "World Class" musicians. Talented people have developed their talent because they enjoy what they do, over the years they have associated with others in their trade or craft, and practiced, practiced, practiced.

As practicing Christians, we are called to witness, teach, and prepare a place for those new to the faith, children, and even those whom we do not yet know. Some of us will be long gone before some of those for whom we prepare even arrive. It is by our faith we accept the call, we fellowship and share our lives with other Christians, and we practice, practice, and practice. By our faith, we are willing to sacrifice that others may know Christ, and accept his words when he said:

Mark 16:15 "Go into all the world and preach the good news to all creation. And in Matthew 28: 19 Therefore go and make disciples of all nations, baptizing them in the name of the Father and of the Son and of the Holy Spirit, 20 and teaching them to obey everything I have commanded you. And surely, I am with you always, to the very end of the age."

James wrote in *James 2: 15-18 Suppose a brother or sister is without clothes and daily food. If one of you says to him, "Go, I wish you well; keep warm and well fed," but does nothing about his physical needs, what good is it? In the same way, faith by itself, if it is not accompanied by action, is dead. But someone will say, "You have faith; I have deeds." Show me your faith without deeds, and I will show you my faith by what I do."*

Practicing Christians work together, helping the less experienced, sharing with those in need, showing love and concern, praying, giving what we can when we can, showing our faith but being careful not to get so wrapped up in church work that we forget the work of the church.

"Father in Heaven, when we pass by a brother who needs help, without seeing his need, pinch us, or whatever we need to wake up to the needs of our neighbor. AMEN"

Newness of Life

The days are getting longer and the temperature is slowly rising. It's been a couple of weeks since I saw a big flock of Blackbirds migrating north, early morning bird songs fill the air, and fat squirrels are playing everywhere. An Armadillo is trying to make his home under my little shop and Rusty, the dog, has been lying in the sun on the little rise above the garage. The Tulip tree, Forsythia and Daffodil blooms have come and gone. Dogwoods, Azaleas, Tulips and a few other spring bloomers are lighting up the landscape as the grass and trees turn green. Last year's little girls now look like young women and the little boys who thought girls were yucky last year are starting to look at them with a new eye. Spring is in the air and all of God's creation is in renewal.

I wonder if the Garden of Eden was like that. Maybe that's where the adage started, "The grass is always greener on the other side of the fence."

In Deuteronomy *11:11 "But the land you are crossing the Jordan to take possession of is a land of mountains and valleys that drinks rain from heaven. 12 It is a land the LORD your God cares for; the eyes of the LORD your God are continually on it from the beginning of the year to its end. 13 So if you faithfully obey the commands I am giving you today–to love the LORD your God and to serve him with all your heart and with all your soul–14 then I will send rain on your land in its season, both autumn and spring rains, so that you may gather in your grain, new wine and oil. 15 I will provide grass in the fields for your cattle, and you will eat and be satisfied."*

In James *5:7-8 "Be patient then brothers, until the Lord's coming. See how the farmer waits for the land to yield its valuable crop and how patient he is for the autumn and spring rains. You too, be patient and stand firm, because the Lord's coming is near.*

Easter is our promise of spring. Believe and we shall surely see the new spring, one that will last forever.

"Thank you Father for the gift of new life given to us through your son Jesus Christ. AMEN"

The Tools of a Christian

With the passing of time I have accumulated a lot of tools. Some were my father's, some my grandfather's and my wife's grandfather's. I have bought many. Some of the older tools I have were picked up at garage sales. For instance, I have a "Can't Hook" that was my grandfather in-law's that I use to roll large logs up on my log splitter. A year or so ago I found a Peavey. That's a can't hook with a spike on the end for breaking up river ice. There are many excellent old ways of doing things that still work. For instance, a triangle with sides of three, four and five forms 90 degrees and can be used for a square. For a perfectly vertical line hang a conical weight on a string and you have a plumb line.

After the death of Solomon, his son led the kingdom into chaos and rebellion. The kingdom divided. Ten tribes moved north, becoming so corrupt they were lost forever. Then the two southern tribes were taken into captivity and Nehemiah became a personal servant of King Artaxerxes.

In Nehemiah 1:1 he says, *"While I was in the fortress city of Susa, [2] Hanani, one of my brothers, came with some other men from Judah. I asked them about the Jews who had escaped and survived the captivity, and about Jerusalem. [3] They told me, "Those in the province who survived the captivity are in great trouble and shame! The wall around Jerusalem is broken down, and its gates have been destroyed by fire!"*

The king had compassion for Nehemiah and released him to return and rebuild the walls and gates. With only a handful of men and encountering much opposition Nehemiah rebuilt the walls and gates. Their tools were ancient and crude but their work was skilled and precision. Is this a story about building walls or building a people? Many people would be coming and place needed to be made for these new people yet to come, so, God gave them the tools they needed.

"Lord, you have given us the tools to do your work. The tools of love, compassion, forgiveness, mercy, kindness, faith, and your grace. Teach us to use these tools for the building of your kingdom. AMEN"

Be There When You Can

Ernie was walking along-side a construction project in a big city and fell into a deep hole. The hole had straight smooth sides with no irregular features for footholds and there was nothing he could stack to help him climb out. All he could do was yell for help. A doctor walked by and Ernie yelled, "Hey Doc. I can't get out. Give me some help." So, the doctor wrote him a prescription and threw it into the hole, but he still couldn't get out. A little later a priest came by and again Ernie yelled up, "Hey Father. Give me some help. I can't get out." So, the priest wrote a prayer and tossed it into the hole, but Ernie still couldn't get out. After a while a stranger walked by and Ernie said, "Hey friend, please help me out of this hole."

So, the man said, OK," and jumped down into the hole with Ernie.

To which Ernie said, "Now what are we going to do? We are both stuck in the hole."

But the man said, "No. Follow me. I have been down here before and I know the way out."

Mary was in her mid-sixties, sitting in the surgery waiting room by herself, twisting a white handkerchief as she waited while her husband was having surgery. It was her first hospital experience and she was afraid.

To Ann's family, surgery was old hat. They laughed and talked as they waited for the doctor's report. Ann noticed Mary, went over and sat by her side and just visited. Mary began to talk and her fears subsided. Ann offered prayer and asked God for comfort. She saw an opportunity where she could be of comfort and simply sat, listened and offered to pray with her.

If we receive the chance, we need to be there for others, comforting them as God has comforted us.

II Corinthians 1:4 *"We offer the same comfort that we ourselves received from God."*

"Lord, be with us that we might show kindness and comfort to others who are in the need. Shine a light on our path that we might see the way we can help. AMEN"

Some People Are Different Than Me

A few weeks ago, an ESL English teacher became ill and was out of school for over a week. I was given her job for three classes a day of Mexican ninth graders, most of whom had been in the U.S. less than six months. The teacher's lesson plans ran out and I spoke no more Spanish than they did English. My Spanish-speaking aide helped conjure up more lessons. We had them write in English a paragraph on where they would go in a time machine. They could go to any time and place? What is your greatest dream? What kind of work would your parents do? What do you want most for your family? Where would you rather be, more than any other place? The most popular answers were: Back to Jesus' day so I could meet and hear him and see his miracles. I want my daddy to work less hours so he could be home more. He is a tree trimmer, or mechanic, or construction worker. My mother cleans motels or works in a cafeteria. I would like for all of my family to be together and not part here and part in Mexico. I want to go back to Mexico and be with my grandmother and friends.

These kids cling together in small groups and an all-Mexican class is more respectful of the teacher and better behaved than the American kids. Last week I had a few classes of kids a little older who had been born here in the United States. However, all of their parents had come here from Mexico. I asked them why their parents moved here. The answer was universal. "My dad can't make enough money for us to live in Mexico." We talked some about church. I thought most of them would be Catholic but they were from a variety of denominations.

Like most people, I have been isolated within my own culture, attending my church, living in my community, and shopping on my side of town. Everything I do is with people who are like me.

Our communities are full of many languages and a lot of cultures. What should we do? Get to know each other, don't fight, play nice.

Mark 16:15 *Jesus said to them, "Go into the whole world and proclaim the good news to every creature."*

"Lord help us to love and respect others who are different from us. MEN"

How far can a squirrel leap?

When we moved to East Texas I built a bluebird house, put it on a post in the middle of a flowerbed, and for several years enjoyed watching bluebirds come every spring and raise their young. A couple of years ago, I did away with the flowerbed and moved the birdhouse. The birds quit coming and I attributed it to location. Then I noticed squirrels playing on the house and my wife said she had seen them leap the six or eight feet from a tree to the top of the house. Sure enough! One day I watched a squirrel cling to the tree, screw up his courage and with a leap of faith land on top of the birdhouse. Only then did it dawn on me that the birds wouldn't nest where the squirrels could get to the house. A few weeks ago, I took the house down, cleaned and repaired it, moved it about 30 feet from the tree and put a squirrel guard on the post. How far will a squirrel's faith let him leap? I don't know, but 30 feet is too far.

How far will your faith let you leap? How big of a chance are you willing to take? Our youngest grand-daughter is in the 4th grade, small for her age, a little over 40 lbs., and is the "flyer" on a cheer team where the other girls are big, strong, high school girls. She seems to have absolute faith in the big girls as they toss her high in the air above a pyramid of girls. We enter into marriage with faith in the one we love. We have faith in the company for which we work.

If I have faith in a God whom I cannot see, faith in Christ whom I never met, and faith in a church founded on faith, how big of a leap have I taken? What do I have to gain except my eternal life? And even if I do not always agree, what do I have to lose if I put my faith in God.

Luke 17:5-6 The apostles said to the Lord, "Increase our faith!" The Lord replied, "If you had faith the size of a mustard seed, you could say to this mulberry tree, 'Be uprooted and planted in the sea,' and it would obey you.

"Father, we have faith in you that you are the one true God, creator of all things, all people, and the one who has given your son Jesus for the forgiveness of our sins. AMEN"

OK, So I'm Average

There was a story on TV about a nine-year-old boy with a 200 plus I.Q. who is holding his own in college. He seems pretty well rounded for a nine-year-old with his brainpower. What struck me about him was his answer to the question, "Do you consider yourself a genius?" His answer was, "No. I consider myself to be gifted, and when God gives you a gift like this you have a responsibility to use it.

At nine I was more concerned with Captain Midnight, the Lone Ranger, and Superman. My interest was sending box tops and a dime for a Captain Midnight decoder ring or a Tom Mix badge. Most kids today aren't that much different. I thought the days of premiums and slogans were long gone until recently. Our youngest granddaughter got some really great buys from a fund-raising thing at school. To the best of my knowledge, she has gotten a voice catcher, which is a battery-operated voice recorder, a crime scene investigator, and I'm not real sure how that works, and a cash machine which operates on her personal credit card to protect the money that she has hidden in her sock drawer or other secret place. She is a really good kid and makes good grades in school but like grandpa she is pretty much average.

Moses gave the Children of Israel these words found in Deuteronomy 6.

6:5 *Love the* LORD *your God with all your heart, all your being, and all your strength.* [6] *These words that I am commanding you today must always be on your minds.* [7] *Recite them to your children. Talk about them when you are sitting around your house and when you are out and about, when you are lying down and when you are getting up.*

We also should teach our children. Give them bible heroes and teach them to love God and obey his commands. Do it with repetition. Teach at home, use devotionals, pray together, attend Sunday school and Church as a family.

"Thank you Father for the church you gave through your son Jesus. AMEN"

About My All Time Super Hero

There was a silent auction at a spaghetti dinner fundraiser for our youth. Two of our men were bidding against each other in an auction for a blue and white cap with Oreo 3 on it. It was commemorative cap for the Stock Car driving hero Dale Earnhardt killed in a crash.

Our granddaughter went to her gymnastic competition in Dallas a day early this week so she could watch her heroes on the Elite teams perform.

When I was about ten I had a comic book collection. My friends and I would get together on some one's front steps to swap books and read the exciting stories of our comic book heroes.

Flying ace and hero Capt. Eddy Rickenbacker landed at the airport and my grandfather took us to see him. Like in the movies, he wore a leather jacket and had a scarf around his neck with one end blowing in the breeze.

9-11 has made us aware of the everyday heroes we often take for granted like the firemen, policeman and just the people next door.

Moms are heroes when they do things like bring you the homework at ten in the morning when you left it home, to keep you from failing your math, and Dads can be heroes because they can fix anything from a broken wagon to a broken heart. Grandmas are heroes because they bake cookies and snuggle good and grandpas because they let you sit on their lap and play with their computer.

The Apostle Paul told us who our all-time hero was when he said in Romans 8:38-39:

[38] *I'm convinced that nothing can separate us from God's love in Christ Jesus our Lord: not death or life, not angels or rulers, not present things or future things, not powers* [39] *or height or depth, or any other thing that is created.*

"Father, thank you for giving to us the greatest hero to ever walk your earth. AMEN"

I Sure Would Like to Be One

I've never seen a purple cow and hope to never see one, but I can tell you here and now, I'd rather see than be one. Have you ever seen an angel? Well, I quite often see one, and I can tell you here and now I'd rather be than see one.

Have you ever seen an angel? I'll bet you have. Think about it. Angels can most often be identified on sight by their pleasant, friendly and cheerful personality. They love children, find fault in no-one, and are always looking for something helpful to do. They are very pleasant to be around and make great friends. They smile a lot, are kind and thoughtful and pleasant in conversation because they are usually more concerned about you than with themselves.

Angels are found just about everywhere. They hold doors and even when they have a cart full of groceries, they let you ahead with your three or four items, they hold a line of traffic while you get out of your parking space, and wave when they drive by.

Angels like to teach Sunday School, sing in the choir, go to youth camp, go on mission trips, visit church visitors and home bound people, and attend church regularly. But, not all angels do all these things nor are all who do these things necessarily angels.

The apostle Paul called what angels do, love. He said:

1Corinthians 13:4-7 *Love is patient, love is kind, it isn't jealous, it doesn't brag, it isn't arrogant, [5] it isn't rude, it doesn't seek its own advantage, it isn't irritable, it doesn't keep a record of complaints, [6] it isn't happy with injustice, but it is happy with the truth. [7] Love puts up with all things, trusts in all things, hopes for all things, endures all things.*

"Lord, I've never seen a real honest to goodness angel but would you help me be an earth bound one? AMEN"

Oh, I remember It Well

Reminiscing seems to be part of the human nature. Most of my good old days are reminiscing about children, especially my grandchildren. Our oldest granddaughter was about six when she asked me what "I love you" meant. I told her it meant that you were very special to me and I liked you a whole lot. After thinking for a few minutes, she said, "Grandpa I love you."

Now she is a teenager. At last year's UMM garage sale I was sitting in a lawn chair by the clothing area when she came over, plopped down on me and started rattling about something she and her daddy were doing. I said, "When did you get so pretty and smart?"

Without hesitation, she said, "One day when you were asleep in front of the TV."

When a former pastor's daughter was about three, she invited one of her friends to church. A few weeks later the whole family joined and are very active in our church life; another "Good Old Day".

Christmas fellowship dinner was a gem. Santa did some research, (Talked to the parents ahead of time), and got information about all of the four to seven-year old's. He had his good-and-bad list and knew what they wanted. Surprise, Surprise.

Remember when new members became active in the church because we invited them, SS classes grew with new families, the children's choir sang, and the youth sent health kits and flood buckets to UMCOR?

Luke 18:15-17 *People were bringing babies to Jesus so that he would bless them. When the disciples saw this, they scolded them. Then Jesus called them to him and said, "Allow the children to come to me. Don't forbid them, because God's kingdom belongs to people like these children. I assure you that whoever doesn't welcome God's kingdom like a child will never enter it."*

"Father, help us to teach the children, that as they grow in stature, they will grow in memories of you. AMEN"

It Will Be Good

When our youngest granddaughter was a toddler, I purchased a stuffed dog named Wishbone for our toy box, because Wishbone was one of her favorite T.V. shows. He is a dreamer, always saving the day and saying about every situation, "This is good!" In one of his dreams his job was to load the king's guns. Once he didn't get the gun latched properly and when the king fired the gun it backfired, blowing off his thumb. Wishbone remarked as usual, "This is good!" To which the king became angry and sent his friend Wishbone to jail.

Later, the king was hunting, and was captured by cannibals. They bound him to a stake and while setting fire to the wood, noticed that the king was missing a thumb. Being superstitious, they sent him on his way.

On his way home, the king remembered how he lost his thumb and felt remorse for the treatment of his friend. He went immediately to the jail to speak with him. "You were right," he said, "it was good that my thumb was blown off." And he told his friend all that had happened. "I am so sorry for sending you to jail. That was bad."

"No," said Wishbone, "It was good!"

"What do you mean, 'It was good'? I sent you to Jail for a year?"

Wishbone answered, "If not in jail, I would have been with you, and that was good."

A Canaanite woman was shouting for mercy. Jesus didn't respond, but finally replied that he had been sent only to the lost sheep of Israel. She knelt before him and begged, "Lord, help me."

In Matthew 15:26-28 He *replied, "It is not good to take the children's bread and toss it to dogs."*

27 She said, "Yes, Lord. But even the dogs eat the crumbs that fall off their masters' table."

28 Jesus answered, "Woman, you have great faith. It will be just as you wish." And right then her daughter was healed.

"Lord, we know that if our faith is strong enough you will always answer and it will be good. AMEN"

And God Created Life

Psalms 104:18 *"The high hills are a refuge for the wild goats; and the rocks for the conies,"* and Proverbs 30:26 *"The Conies are but a feeble folk, yet make they their houses in the rocks.*

We live in the piney woods of East Texas but it's also home to many oaks and where there's oaks there's squirrels. Our yard has many oaks with squirrels in abundance. They chase each other up and down and around the trees and scamper along the limbs jumping from one tree to another. After playtime, they seem to spend the rest of the day eating acorns or up in their nests asleep.

It's been said that when the wild animals really fatten up in the fall it's going to be a hard, hard winter. Now that's either just an "Old Wives' Tale" or we still have hard winter coming because the squirrels are really fat. Yesterday I watched a squirrel on the bank beside our drive spinning an acorn in his paws, his little mouth chomping away. He was so fat he looked like a little Buddha sitting on his haunches.

Of the birds, Jesus said in Matthew 6:25-27 *"Therefore I tell you, do not worry about your life, what you will eat or what you will drink, or about your body, what you will wear. Is not life more than food, and the body more than clothing? Look at the birds of the air; they neither sow nor reap nor gather into barns, and yet your heavenly Father feeds them. Are you not of more value than they?"*

If you wonder where I'm going with all of this animal talk it's just this: There is so much to be learned from animals; the sheer joy of living, playing, hard work, rest, survival and loyalty.

And since God put us in charge of all his creation, there is much required of us, like worshiping Him, loving Him, and serving Him, and most of all, spreading His "Good News" to all the world.

"Father, thank you for the animals over which you have put us in charge. Guide us that we might be as true, as selfless, and as free of worry in our lives as they. AMEN"

Maybe it Will Snow

There hasn't been much snowfall for a while. We moved to East Texas on February the 19th several years ago, and had an ice storm to greet us the next day. Since then, to my recollection, there's been two other storms, one knocked out our electricity for a few days. And then there was one light snowfall, making the neighborhood kids really work to make snowmen. We'll get some good snowfall one of these days when weather is just right.

My brother-in-law who lives in Pennsylvania came to visit us over Christmas several years ago because he wanted to celebrate a nice warm and sunny Christmas. There were three snows before Christmas that year, and the last one was a record eight inches. Two days later it thawed a little and then a really cold front came in and froze all the slush and wet snow. He swore he would never come to Texas and freeze again.

Our yards that were fresh and green only a few weeks ago, are beginning to turn their winter brown. I know that spring will burst forth in full color and restore all green life but my patience is kind of like a child waiting for mom and dad to get up on Christmas morning.

However, there is one beautiful, magnificent, and glorious winter scene to which I always look forward. A layer of only an inch or so of new fallen snow covers the brown and bareness of winter. Even an ice storm, breaking trees and power lines, has an infinite charm. On a morning of new fallen snow, I stand at my window dreading the first tracks that spoil the winter scene. Of course, the thicker the layer of snow the more beautiful the landscape. I wish there were a way the snow could fall on all the fields and lawns but not on the streets and roads.

The love of God is like a new fallen snow, covering all of the brown and unlovely-ness. No matter how bad the week, no matter how hard the times, worshiping God and sharing in the fellowship of the church is like a blanket of new fallen snow. As we study, worship and fellowship together I know I am not alone and God's world is a lovely place.

Psalm 147:16 *"God spreads snow like it was wool; God scatters frost like it was ashes;"*

"Thank you, God, for the beauty you put in nature. AMEN"

World Class

We belong to the Tyler Community Concert Association. Concerts give us a night out, a time to hone our culture, increase our couth, and enjoy a couple of hours of entertainment. Richard Glazier was a performer a couple of years ago, and I was a little apprehensive. A one-person performance gets boring by the end of a two-hour program and as much as I love sweets I can only eat so much pecan pie or chocolate fudge. But, this night was an exception. At an early age, Glazier became obsessed with the Steinway piano. An obsession extending all through music but especially the popular music of the 30s, 40s, and 50s. As he played he told us the history of George and Ira Gershwin, of Janet McDonald, Judy Garland, Fred Astaire, and Oscar Hammerstein. He told of unknown musicians who worked behind the sound stages. By the end of the concert I had pleasantly grown in music appreciation. We headed for the side door and as we passed the orchestra pit Mr. Glazier was retrieving the electronic gear he used with his show. "Thank you." I said as we passed him.

With all sincerity, he said, "Thank you for letting me present it." Sometimes when I watch a performer or athlete I wonder if I totally devoted myself to the task and diligently practiced and practiced could I have been that good. I am convinced that in some area, if I had put heart and soul in it, devoted my life to it; I may have become "World class" at something. Then......maybe not. Maybe I could have been a world class dad, or a world class husband or cook or gardener.

Peter and Paul were world class church leaders but try as I might, that level is beyond me. Maybe some of those silent ones who quietly serve without waving banners, without noise, those who do God's work and wait without pay or praise, those Mother Teresa's who serve others.

Matthew 25:35-36 *For I was hungry and you gave me something to eat, I was thirsty and you gave me something to drink, I was a stranger and you invited me in, I needed clothes and you clothed me, I was sick and you looked after me, I was in prison and you came to visit me*

"Lord help me to be a world class Christian, AMEN"

Strangers and Three Word Phrases

I drink a lot of milk and every few days I stop at Braum's to pick up a couple of gallons. Mary waits on me. I know her name because she wears a nametag. She knows mine because I too wear a nametag. Our conversations are short, usually about grandkids.

My wife, daughter and I were on the New York subway a few years ago, and were looking at our map trying to decide where our stop would be to get off at The Cloisters. A lady standing next to us said quietly, "Put away that map and tell me where you want to go. Everyone here will know you are tourists." Her directions were better than the map.

Does it really hurt so much to talk to strangers? "What was the name of the clerk that checked you out at the grocery, or the waitress that served your lunch?" They probably had on nametags. What about glancing at their nametag and saying, "How's Bill today?" or "How's Sarah's day going?"

Three word phrases are easy to use. Think of some of the ones you like. It makes one feel as if the person or business we are dealing with is so kind, and well, sort of human. And, after a particularly long and boring speech isn't it nice to hear, "And in conclusion". There are many really good three-word starter phrases like "How are you," and, "You're looking well." Of course, both need to be accompanied with a smile and a twinkle.

Hebrews 13:2, *"Do not neglect to show hospitality to strangers, for by doing that some have entertained angels without knowing it."*

If someone doesn't look so good, how about "are you OK?" And if you are asked, how about "I am fine." Be careful if you pray. The answer may come from some other three-word phrases like "can I help?" or "May I help?" or "let me help". So, mean it when you pray for them. In Matthew 25 Jesus gave us a whole list of three-word phrases;

"I was hungry - you fed me, I was thirsty - you gave water, I was a stranger - you welcomed me. I was naked - you clothed me. I was sick - you nursed me. I was in prison - you visited me."

Some three-word phrases may be hard to say like "Maybe you're right, I am wrong, I am sorry, please excuse me, and the tough one, It's my fault." Don't use "Just call me if I can do anything." They will never call.

"Dear Lord, put the right words in my mouth. AMEN"

Can it be Fixed

At summer camp a group of kids were separated into two teams. Each team was given a tube of toothpaste and a Styrofoam bowl. They were told that on GO they were to squeeze as much toothpaste as possible out of the tube and into the bowl. Each team squeezed, twisted and milked their tube until they were virtually dry. They finished at almost the same time and each team thought they were first, but the contest wasn't over. Now they were told to put all of the toothpaste back in the tube. Everything was tried. A boy in one group put toothpaste in his mouth and blew it into the tube. It didn't work. The other group was more innovative. They looked through their packs for tools. One boy had a scout knife and a girl had a spoon. They cut the bottom seam of the tube open, found a stick on the ground to round out the inside of the tube and then used the spoon to reload the toothpaste. Except for the coating of toothpaste on the spoon and stick they managed to get virtually all of the toothpaste back in the tube. After a little clean up the tube was folded over on the end and although somewhat battered was a full tube of toothpaste. But, even then it just wasn't the same.

In the seventies was a song called McArthur Park? There was a picnic, the weather changed and the cake got left out in the rain. No matter what was done to the cake, dried out and re-iced or whatever, it would never be the same again.

On the TV series "Judging Amy" a schoolteacher neighbor was wrongly accused by an angry teen of child molestation. He was cleared in court but still had to leave town. Doubt would be forever over his head.

Gossip, rumors, doubts, and lies may all be proven wrong, and mistakes repaired, but things are never quite the same. God's law is for good reason.

Ex 20:16 *"You shall not bear false witness against your neighbor."*

"Thank you Lord for the teachings and examples in the scripture. AMEN"

Our Basic Needs Never Change

The summer between my second and third grade we moved to a house with a path out back to a new WPA privy, a good well and pump, room for chickens, a cow and calf, a hog pen and a big garden. There was a big farmhouse across the road with a big barn and big barn lot.

One day I was out front when the biggest tractor I'd ever seen, with steel wheels taller than a man that crunched on the gravel as it lumbered along. It was pulling a huge machine that looked as big as the barn across the road. Men were walking along with it, and four more had come ahead to open the gate into the barn lot. They also dug out a section of fence so the gate opening was twice as big. With great difficulty, the big machine was turned and twisted into the barn lot, blocked up, and a long-galvanized tube swung on a boom out away from the machine. A wide flat drive belt was connected from the tractor to the machine and when the tractor was started the machine whined and whirred.

The next morning a long line of wagons, some pulled by horses or mules and some by tractors, was lined up to the machine, each loaded with shocks of wheat. What it was, was a threshing machine. The wheat was fed into the machine, straw blew out the galvanized tube and eventually made a mountain of straw, and the golden grains of wheat poured down into a reservoir.

I grew and was allowed to drive the mules to mow and to cultivate crops and then drive the tractor when I was able to hand crank it and work its hand lift accessories. I hated milking and feeding but since the day I fell in love with that threshing machine I have loved any kind of equipment. Things on the farm have changed, as have things on all jobs. We have come a long way since a twelve-year-old drove a team of mules.

But, the need for a young boy to be in Sunday school and church is just as necessary today as is God's forgiving grace. The need for prayer and the corporate worship of God, existed then, now, and always will.

1 Corinthians 14:26; *"When you meet together, each one has a psalm, a teaching, a revelation, a tongue, or an interpretation. All these things must be done to build up the church."*

"Thank You God for the wisdom and experience of our elders, AMEN."

The Eleventh Commandment

Jesus said to his disciples: John 13:34 *"A new command I give you: Love one another. As I have loved you, so you must love one another.* [35] *By this all men will know that you are my disciples, if you love one another."*

One afternoon while in Houston at the Texas Annual Conference, we were leaving the hotel. The van was parked next to a grassy median and while my friend Jason was getting in the driver's side I walked up the median, tripped over my own feet, rolled as I went down ending up on the grass like a big June bug with all four in the air. With bad knees, I sometimes fall and have gotten used to rolling as I go down. My main concern was, "Did I get any grass stains on my trousers?"

And then there was a face directly over me. It was my friend Sam Daffin, his face showing great concern, fear, and love for a friend. He asked if I was OK as he extended his hand to give me a lift up. Now I am sure that Sam would have done the same for anyone but that day it wasn't just anyone he was helping. It was me. When I became the object of concern and assistance from a friend it put things in a different perspective. I wasn't doing my Christian duty but observing someone else doing a good deed. And, in this case, it was I being the recipient of love and concern. *"As I have loved you, so you must love one another. By this all men will know that you are my disciples, if you love one another."*

Church is the best place I know for Christians to practice loving one another.

"Father in Heaven, teach us to love as you have loved us." AMEN

All You Have to Do Is Ask

The other evening, as we watched America's funniest home videos, there was a segment on wedding proposals. An airplane was pulling a sign that said, "Will you marry me," another was a majorette being proposed to on the 50-yard line, one proposal was on a lighted bill-board across from where a girl was eating lunch and, well, you get the message. Marriage just doesn't get under way without someone asking the all-important question. The three characters in Longfellow's poem, "The Courtship of Miles Standish, are Miles Standish, Priscilla Mullins, and John Alden. Standish is too proud to ask Priscilla and asks Alden to propose for him. Priscilla asks John, "Why don't you speak for yourself John?" He does, and they do.

Asking comes many ways. Sometimes even as a statement. My mother used to say, "Lee pick up your clothes, go to the garden and get me some fresh tomatoes, the lawn needs mowing and dozens of other requests. That's the way moms and wives do. It's still asking.

Asking is such a simple chore, yet most of us fear it. Are we afraid of rejection? Making fools of ourselves? Or is it that we are just not sure how we should ask. Maybe we should just put our best foot forward and say, "Would you -and then say it.

In Matthew 7:7 Jesus said, "*Ask, and you will receive. Search, and you will find. Knock, and the door will be opened to you.*" In Matthew 7:8 "*For everyone who asks, receives. Whoever seeks, finds. And to everyone who knocks, the door is opened.*" And in Revelation 3:20 "*Look! I'm standing at the door and knocking. If any hear my voice and open the door, I will come in to be with them, and will have dinner with them, and they will have dinner with me.*"

How difficult is it to ask, "Do you have a church home? Come to our fellowship dinner with me, bring the whole family, visit our Sunday school class, our men's group, women's group, or youth hang time."

Just say, "Would you - - - - - - - - - - - - - - - - - -" and then say it.

"Lord, you asked us. Teach us to ask others. AMEN"

Honk

When I was a boy we lived near a small town away from businesses and freeways. It was a rural farm area, a few miles from any big city. In the fall, when the first cool weather descended on us, a honking, honking, honking could be heard in the distant sky. The sound would grow louder and louder until a V formation appeared from the distance. We were on the annual migration route of the Canadian geese, and as winter approached they formed groups heading south to a warmer climate, and in the spring, they came north toward home. Sometimes you could see two or three formations at a time. At night, I'd lay awake, listening to them flying through the night, wondering; where do they come from, and where do the go? On a moonlit night, as they honked their way through, you could see their formation framed against the sky. When the geese are in formation the honking encourages all to stay in tight formation, keep up, and press on. Each goose drafts off of the goose in front of him and flight is made easier. In their V formation, the flock can travel more than two-thirds farther without resting than a single bird in lone flight. When the lead bird begins to tire, it drops back and the next bird takes the lead. If a bird is shot or becomes sick and falls, two geese follow it down and stay with it until it's well or dies. The two or three, take flight and fly, drafting off of each other, and rotating positions until they catch their flock or join another.

On Sunday morning, I'm standing near the coffee pot and someone comes up, extends a hand, and says, "Good morning. How'd the week go?" He's really honking. We're really saying, "How are you friend? How are you doing? I've missed you." Women get a hug, and men get a shake or sometimes a hug. That's the way we do. We honk to keep each other going. If you've done all you can do, and still need help, be a goose, honk. Everything being said, stay in formation, keep honking.

Matthew 6:26 Look at the birds in the sky. They don't sow seed or harvest grain or gather crops into barns. Yet your heavenly Father feeds them. aren't you worth much more than they are?

"Father in Heaven, thank you for the fellowship of the church and fellow Christians. AMEN"

Howdy

A couple of years ago, our daughter lost her purse, in of all places a New York taxi. A few days later she received it in the mail. A note with it said, "Lady, you left your purse in my cab. I kept out the money it took to mail it back to you. It was simply signed, Taxi Driver. The postage was $2.40, the exact amount missing from the purse. When we talked to her a few months later, she was writing a note to a teenage girl whose purse she had found on the subway.

There have been so many strangers who have helped me, befriended me, and gone out of their way to be kind.

Have you ever walked down an avenue in a large city, perhaps window shopping, or like me just gawking? The sidewalks are big and wide but crowded with people. The people you meet are hurrying away from where you're going, and the ones walking your way are talking about shopping, or golf, or their work, but most are silent. This crowd, this mob of people, just don't seem friendly, but in truth, the only way to have privacy in a crowd is to ignore everyone around you.

We're used to country folk and country ways, where every pickup driver waves, and people say "howdy." Sometimes people need a little shove to be friendly. When I'm shopping, I try to say hello to every person I meet. Lots of times it brings about a brief but pleasant conversation.

In Romans 12:13 Paul says, *"Contribute to the needs of God's people, and welcome strangers into your home. "3* John 1:5 stresses_helping strangers. *"Dear friend, you act faithfully in whatever you do for our brothers and sisters, even though they are strangers,"* and Hebrews 13:1-2 says, *"Keep loving each other like family. ² Don't neglect to open up your homes to guests, because by doing this some have been hosts to angels without knowing it."*

Finders keepers, loosers, weepers? WWJD. What would Jesus do?

"Thank you Lord that in you we are all one family, even strangers. AMEN"

Let's Visit a Church

I recently read a story by Arthur Caliandro, author, speaker, and pastor to a New York church. A few years ago, he holed up at an inn in the Shenandoah Valley, away from phones, meetings and appointments, to do some writing. On Sunday, he slid into the back pew of the town church. People were greeting one another and sharing bits of news. He said that all of a sudden, he felt lonely being so far from his friends. At the end of the service he stood to put on his overcoat. There was a tap on his shoulder and he turned around to see an elderly lady in her Sunday best. "You're a visitor here," she said. "I'm very glad you came.

He said after all these years he can't recall what the choir sang or the preacher said, but he does remember the woman's kindness to him.

When you are on vacation take along your bible and a devotional book. On Sunday find a church to visit. If you do you can probably tell some similar stories. Once near Orlando, Florida we visited an old frame church. There were two things I remember about the church. One was how we were included and encouraged to talk in the S.S. class we visited and the other was that the sanctuary had no ceiling but an exposed intricate system of Cantilevers and Suspended Spans. The architecture of their little frame church was memorable but it was their kindness that was unforgettable. A church in a small town a few miles west of Atlanta, Georgia had all kinds of questions for us when they discovered we were vacationers from Texas. Another time we happened upon a Charismatic church. We didn't know it until their worship began. I was uncomfortable during the service but afterward the people were delightfully kind and wanted us to stay awhile for their "Dinner on the grounds." Although I've heard many sermons when we have visited I don't remember most of them. But, I remember those kind, gentle and friendly people.

Galatians 5:22 *But the fruit of the Spirit is love, joy, peace, patience, kindness, goodness, and faithfulness.*

They accepted me, and let me know we were friends.

"Lord, sprinkle us with that kind of love. AMEN"

What I've Learned

I don't remember my first day on earth, but I remember learning not to run too fast pulling my baby sister or she would fall out and get hurt. I remember mother wouldn't believe it was my dog, Pal, who got out the scissors and cut the curtains, and that Pal didn't like my vegetables any better than me. I learned "Jesus loves me, this I know," and the Bible sure had a lot of stories and Grandma must know them all.

When I started school, I learned that the nicer I was to people the nicer they were to me, and when we went to church just about everybody was nice. When I was a teen my parents were pretty strict, but even then, they trusted me a lot. I learned what it meant that Jesus died on the cross and I liked my SS class because there were more girls than boys.

As an adult, I've learned the church is an extension of my home and the best place to raise kids. My kids always thought I could do "anything" whether I could or not, and taking my son fishing was more fun than catching the fish, and if I remained silent and listened while chauffeuring my daughter and her friends they appreciated it, and I learned a lot. I did a bang up job of picking a wife, the world's worst drivers follow me everywhere I go, and if someone says something unkind about me, I have to live so that no one will believe it. There are people who love you dearly, but just don't know how to show it, and you could make someone's day with a simple toot of the horn or a "howdy." Children and grandparents are natural allies. No matter how bad it seems, life does go on, and will be better tomorrow. Singing out of the Cokesbury renews my soul. You can tell a lot about your neighbor by the way he keeps his yard, takes his family to church on Sunday and he and his wife come and go together. Regardless of how you got along with your parents, you miss them terribly when they're gone, and making a living is not the same as making a life. And life usually gives you a second chance. I learned that God's creation is visible in a sunset, a newborn baby, a soft gentle breeze, and through the actions of children.

1 Timothy 4:4. *Everything that has been created by God is good, and nothing that is received with thanksgiving should be rejected.*

"Lord, Thank you for the lessons of life. AMEN"

Growth Takes Practice

We pick up our fourth-grade granddaughter after school and keep her until her mother picks her up on her way home from work. When the weather is right, and she has her homework finished, she and I go to the neighbor's pool and swim. We're constantly making up new water games that the two of us can play. I hold up a little "boogie board" and then sail it to the other end of the pool. We pretend that a big wind came up and blew it out of my hand. She saves the day by swimming to the other end of the pool and retrieving it for me. One day she tried standing up on a foam rubber floatation matt but it kept sinking under her feet and she couldn't stay up. Then she had me hold two boogie boards on the matt while she climbed on and stood up. It worked. She stood there wobbling a little, looking straight ahead, and with determination would say, "I can do this. I can do this," until she got her balance. Now she can get up, and have me spin the matt and tow her around the pool without falling.

Concentration and determination are the only ways we have in learning success in life. How many times did young David throw a rock with his sling before he was successful? Eventually he became good enough to kill the giant Goliath. How many times did I try to milk a cow before I could sit on the stool and fill the bucket without my father's help? With a toothless grin and food all over our face we learn to feed ourselves. Association with others who are growing encourages us to grow. This is the way children learn, grow, and become mature adults, but as we become adults we develop ways to stop growing. Things like fear of failure, loss of interest, loss of confidence, fear of embarrassment and fear of change prevent us from further growth.

Scripture advises practice. Luke 2:52, "*And Jesus grew in wisdom and stature, and in favor with God and men.*"

Luke 6:47 Jesus says, "*I will show you what he is like who comes to me and hears my words and puts them into practice*".
Romans 12:13 Paul says, "*Share with God's people who are in need. Practice hospitality.*"

"Lord, lead us to practice love, understanding, humility, and compassion. AMEN"

Round and Round, We Go

A friend asked me, "What makes your church unique to itself and different from all others? Why do people join? Why do they keep coming? Why are they willing to support the church and its ministry?"

My answer; "They say we are a friendly church, we have a lot of love to share, we have a good preacher, and the people like each other."

"True," My friend said, "And that's good, but all churches should be able to say that, and sermons alone don't build and maintain churches. The heart of church growth are its circles. They are the building and support groups. The largest one is the group that worships together. The strongest? That's the one that meets for fellowship before Sunday school and church and goes out for lunch together after church. Stand off and watch them some time. Each person is anxious to see what the other has done in the last week. It has been seven whole days since they last met and there is a lot of catching up to do. Other circles are the men, and women's groups, the youth and children's groups, choir, fellowship dinners, Sunday school, prayer groups and even all of the committees."

The circles are what make the church. You see, there are two ways in; walk in and join or be invited. People respond the best when they are invited. You can start anywhere, fellowship dinner, or any other group, but, the important circle meets every Sunday morning to worship God. But, if that is your only circle you really should consider a few more.

He drew a circle that shut me out ~ Heretic, rebel, a thing to flout. But Love and I had the wit to win, we drew a circle that took him in! "Edwin Markham"

Do you suppose feeding the five thousand may have been the first fellowship dinner? It is recorded in Matthew.

Matthew 14:18, *"Bring them here to me." [19] He ordered the crowds to sit down on the grass. He took the five loaves of bread and the two fish, looked up to heaven, blessed them and broke the loaves apart and gave them to his disciples. Then the disciples gave them to the crowds."* "Thank you Lord for the church, that we may have fellowship, learn, and grow together in your word. AMEN"

Fishing in The Storm

When our son was a teenager, I worked with a man who was an avid crappie fisherman, who fished every chance he had. He knew when, where, and how deep they were running, and always came home with a cooler full. He invited me to bring my son and go with him, so, on a Friday after work he came by with his boat and off we went. About dusk we put in and headed across the lake to where the tops of some tall trees just stuck out of the water. He said they would be running deep around those trees. At dark, we dropped our lines.

We had neglected to check a weather forecast for the area and Just as we got settled in, the wind began to blow until the lake was really white capping. We reeled in, untied the boat and headed for shore. Our course was strait into the wind with waves coming over the windshield. Before long there was enough water in the boat that the gas tanks were floating. In the pitch-black night, we could make out a lone yellow bulb burning on shore and we kept straight for it. We reached a cove and found shelter from the wind before the boat was swamped. We were safe in the cove but there was no sleep that night as the rain poured. At daylight, we were only about a hundred yards from the marina where we had put in. I had fully expected the boat to sink. We had our life jackets and could have hung onto one another and probably been blown back into the tree tops or at worst the far shore. In the daylight, someone would have found us.

Matthew 8:26 *He got up and gave orders to the winds and the lake, and there was a great calm.*

Christ is our life jacket and in the church, we can hang onto one another.

"Lord, we look to you in all the storms of life." AMEN

For Praise of Work Well Done

The pointed end would be the bow of his ship, and a smaller block the ship's cabin. A few missed strikes and he managed to nail his cabin on the middle of his ship. "Look daddy! Look at my boat."

"Yes son, that's a fine ship. You can sail around the world in that." His craftsmanship had been confirmed by his father.

I have a brother and sister who are twins. One time at a church Christmas party they received gifts for twin girls. My sister received a doll and my brother a toy flat iron. One evening the next week a lady came by our house with another toy to be exchanged for the iron, but my brother would have nothing to do with it. The iron was a road maker. He took it across the sandbox leaving a smooth surface the width of the iron and drove his trucks and cars over the road. He was praised for the fine roads he had built and kept the iron.

I have eaten dozens of imaginary cookies, and drunken tea from little imaginary cups. always praising the cook.

In school, we need good grades to confirm that which we have learned, on the job we need promotions, bonuses and praise to confirm that we are doing a good job.

When did you last praise a waitress for her service, thank the mechanic who fixed your car or tell a neighbor how much you appreciate their neighborliness.

Did I thank my wife for shortening my new pants or tell her how good last night's dinner was? I can't remember. I'd best do it.

The scripture confirms what God created was good.

Genesis 1:31 *God saw everything he had made: it was supremely good.*

Luke 3:22 *And there was a voice from heaven: "You are my Son, whom I dearly love; in you I find happiness."*

"Lord, thank you for all you give us, and for your love, forgiveness, and your son Jesus Christ. AMEN"

What's in A Name?

The Texas State Fair wasn't far from where I was raised, and I went every year. I loved the midway with its rides, the sideshows, the automobile building, livestock shows, and sites. In 1952 came Big Tex, 52 feet tall, size 70 boots, and a 75-gallon hat. When Tex talked, his voice thundered over the whole central area of the fairgrounds.

In Bemidji, Minnesota is a statue of Paul Bunyan and his big blue ox, Babe, and in Wisconsin a talking walleyed bass. What would it be like for seven-year-old Billy to hear a huge Paul Bunyan, with his big axe, say in his big booming voice, "Hello, Billy." He almost breaks and runs clear out of Minnesota, with no idea that a man working the crowd gets names, and relays them to the man with the microphone? All he knew was that Paul Bunyan knew his name!

The theme song for the TV sitcom "Cheers" says, "Wouldn't it be nice to go where everybody knows your name?"

Your name is your personal label, and in earlier days a man's name was his bond. A businessman or craftsman that everyone knew by name had to be honest and produce quality work. Deals were struck on a handshake and you could really count on a man with a good name.

In an old Guide Post was a story of a great grandmother who had outlived everyone. Her time was close, and she was ready, but depressed. Then a young great niece figured out her depression. All she needed was to hear her name, one she hadn't heard for many years. So, instead of calling her Auntie, her niece said, "Nancy. You're looking well this morning." And the old lady beamed.

The worst names are the blame names; they, them, whoever, and someone. "Someone ought to align those baskets. They look awful." Sally is the chairperson of the basket committee and we can berate her with or without intending by using the blame name.

Home and church are both places where everyone knows your name, and so does God.

"Lord, as you lead me through life, thank, you that you call me by name," AMEN

Come On, Move It

It seems I always have trouble when I hurry. In fact, one of my favorite sayings is, "The hurrier I go, the behinder I get."

The foreman on a housing project said, "Let's knock this job out and then we're out of here." If it were my house being built I'd just as soon time be taken to insure everything was plumb, true and according to blueprint. Dry cleaning in by ten out by five, photos developed in one hour, Speedy Pantry, Speedy Car Wash, drive through windows; What happened to "Slow down and smell the roses, take the time to do it right, and enjoy doing a good job? Today has reached, "Wham, bam, your good to go."

If I'm having surgery I would rather the doctor didn't knock out the job and get out of there. I like good service, food well prepared, and my car OK when I pick it up from the repair shop.

How is my faith doing? Do I say a quick prayer, roll over and go to sleep, or do I take time to talk to God? Is my bible study just a matter of reading a quick scripture or do I really study it? How about half-hour worship services? What if the Baptists and Presbyterians do beat me to the cafeteria? I surely won't starve.

Our granddaughter's cheer team was out of town for a performance. They stopped at a Denny's for a meal and took time for prayer before they ate. An elderly couple observed them and picked up their $60.00 check. I don't say we should pray for free meals but the incident does show the rarity of a group of teens taking time to pray on their own.

Sunday school is an extra hour each week. Do you have time? While on vacation do you take time to visit a church?

Proverbs 21:5 *"The plans of the diligent end up in profit, but those who hurry end up with loss."*

"Lord help me to take time for your work and do it right. AMEN"

God Is My GPS

One of my friends sells commercial lawn equipment to cities, schools, and golf courses. Recently he got a new diesel truck to deliver his equipment. Inside the truck are all the comforts of home, including a GPS system. Punch an address into the GPS and it would tell him how far it was to his destination, where to turn and lead him there one step at a time. I have other friends who have these. They are fascinating units.

In Acts 9:5-12 *⁵ "Who are you, Lord?" Saul asked.*
"I am Jesus, whom you are persecuting," he replied. ⁶ "Now get up and go into the city, and you will be told what you must do."

⁷ The men traveling with Saul stood there speechless; they heard the sound but did not see anyone. ⁸ Saul got up from the ground, but when he opened his eyes he could see nothing. So they led him by the hand into Damascus. ⁹ For three days he was blind, and did not eat or drink anything.

¹⁰ In Damascus there was a disciple named Ananias. The Lord called to him in a vision, "Ananias!"

"Yes, Lord," he answered.

¹¹ The Lord told him, "Go to the house of Judas on Straight Street and ask for a man from Tarsus named Saul, for he is praying. ¹² In a vision he has seen a man named Ananias come and place his hands on him to restore his sight."

So, one step at a time Saul, whom we now call Paul, was guided through a conversion and became the man who took Jesus' name to the Gentiles and ultimately us.

In Luke 22:8-13 *⁸ Jesus sent Peter and John, saying, "Go and make preparations for us to eat the Passover."*

⁹ "Where do you want us to prepare for it?" they asked.

¹⁰ He replied, "As you enter the city, a man carrying a jar of water will meet you. Follow him to the house that he enters, ¹¹ and say to the owner of the house, 'The Teacher asks: Where is the guest room, where I may eat the Passover with my disciples?' ¹² He will show you a large room upstairs, all furnished. Make preparations there."

"Father, guide us to the place where we should be." AMEN

You Don't Have Kids? Think Again!

Have you ever carried a cat upside down? I never had much luck carrying cats in any position.

The family next door has three children. A boy about eight, another about five, and a little blond headed, blue-eyed girl of about three. When they are playing, the youngest tags along behind, with a miniature wiener dog named Oscar, and carrying one of the kittens, head down and tail in her face. The kitten doesn't seem to mind.

This family is really in the business of raising kids, and doing a good job of it. The old south was good at raising kids. All of the kids called me Mr. Lee instead of Lee and the women would have been called Miss Martha or Miss Mary or whatever fit their given name and there would be a lot of yes mams and yes sirs and all adults treated all children like they were their own. Australian Aborigines are that way. Everyone in the group treats the children as if they were their own. They feed them, love them and dote over them as they grow up to be a gentle people.

Luke 18:15-17 *15 People were also bringing babies to Jesus for him to place his hands on them. When the disciples saw this, they rebuked them. 16 But Jesus called the children to him and said, "Let the little children come to me, and do not hinder them, for the kingdom of God belongs to such as these. 17 Truly I tell you, anyone who will not receive the kingdom of God like a little child will never enter it." Do you know that you have children watching you? Are you ready for that? With the right models, they will grow as Christians, kind, and gentle people, firm in their faith, and, unless you are three, don't try to carry a cat upside down. They will tolerate children but not us.*

"Father, make us aware of our influence on children." AMEN

Dreams and Dreamers

Two little boys were riding their bicycles down a dusty dirt road. About a mile from town they came to a graveyard surrounded by a tall stone wall with a huge pecan tree at its edge. They laid down their bicycles and sat under the tree to rest.

On the other side of the wall two men were dividing pecans. The boys could hear them talking as one would say, two for you, two for me. One boy's eyes got big and he whispered, "Do you hear that? The Lord and the devil are over there dividing souls."

The other said, "I think you're right."

They jumped on their bikes and rode as fast as they could until they met an old man walking with a cane. They told him what they had heard, but the old man told them they had too much imagination. They insisted until he went back to the graveyard with them. As they listened they heard, "These are for you and these are for me."

The old man said, "Boys you may be right."

Just then one of the voices on the other side said, "Well, I guess that's all except for those three nuts over by the big tree." The old man on his cane beat the boys back to town.

Acts 2:17 *"In the last days, God says, I will pour out my Spirit on all people. Your sons and daughters will prophesy, your young men will see visions, your old men will dream dreams."*

A vivid imagination may be silly and unrealistic, or we can dream dreams that improve the world around us. Often, we find that when you stick your head above the crowd, someone will swing at it. So, dream big, and if necessary wear a helmet.

"Father, bless our dreams, and give us the courage to follow them, that we may make our part of the world a better place." AMEN

An Elmer's Glue Religion

My friend broke his fishing rod. He didn't just break off the tip, he slammed the car door on it. There was a four-inch section in several pieces, so, being a thrifty man, he decided to fix it. He laid his fishing pole on the kitchen table and examined it. All of the pieces were there. None were missing. Tape wouldn't work, and it was too small to clamp metal around, so he decided to glue it. He got a bottle of Elmer's glue and went to work, propping pieces up and holding pieces down until all was in alignment. With his tongue in the corner of his mouth and his glasses way down on his nose he began to apply glue. He soaked glue into every broken crack and when it dried he built it up to give it more strength. When the rod was thoroughly dry, it was a masterpiece. Maybe it was even better than when it was new.

The next Saturday morning he took it to the lake for a trial run. He cast a few yards out into the lake and when he reeled in his line the end dipped into the water. Within a couple of minutes, the rod was in pieces. It hadn't dawned on him that Elmer's glue was water-soluble. When the rod was dunked, the glue dissolved.

You were out of church for three weeks, not unusual for you, but this time you were hospitalized. No one came by, not even the preacher. You just assumed that somehow everyone would know?

You just aren't a Sunday school person and you can worship God in a sunset across the lake.

If either of the above fit, your faith may be put together with Elmer's glue.

A strong faith will be shown by your actions. Get involved and switch to God's waterproof faith or keep on like you are, but you will have to stay out of the water.

James said in, 2:20 *"Are you so slow? Do you need to be shown that faith without actions has no value at all?"*

"Lord, give me a strong waterproof faith and help me to be faithful. AMEN"

Life Changes

A long time ago, when I was a boy, my room had been added to the rear of the house, where I had a bed, dresser, and straight back chair I used for a table. On it I had an old wood cabinet, table model radio. There was no heat, and on cold nights I piled on the covers. In the summer, I slept with my windows open and woke at first light. I'd pull on a pair of shorts, no shirt, no shoes and out the back door I'd go. My dog Teddy slept on the porch, and we were off to discover the day.

I had set some chicken eggs under a guinea hen for her to hatch and raise. Guineas make good mothers but they haven't a lick of sense. If I clapped my hands or shouted, the guinea hen would fly straight up, landing thirty or more feet away, in high grass, looking frantically for her peeps, while the they were looking for her. Then I'd scoot her babies toward her, till they were re-united.

I loved to drive the tractor and pretty well kept up with plowing and cultivating. I rigged an old generator on the tractor's belt pulley to run lights so I could plow at night. I got fussed for going swimming in the afternoon and plowing half the night. Our neighbor often needed an extra tractor and hand, which paid well. That helped at home and still gave me spending money to take my younger brother and sisters to see Gene Autrey or Roy Rogers.

Life was easy. I ate well, slept well, and enjoyed being alone. School, church and family reunions were enough social life.

Paul said in 1 Cor. 13:11 *"When I was a child, I used to speak like a child, reason like a child, think like a child. But now that I have become a man, I've put an end to childish things."*

Back then, no one depended on me, today they do. Then, I had no responsibilities, now I do. Today I have knowledge and today I am expected to pass that knowledge on. Today I have gifts and today I am required to share. Today I have been forgiven, so today I must forgive, today I have been loved and today I must love. Today I am a man, and today I must put childish ways behind me."

"As I grow Lord, make me better, that I might serve you through serving others. AMEN"

Times of Disaster

Was Elijah the first meteorologist?

I Kings 18:41. *And Elijah said to Ahab, "Go, eat and drink, for there is the sound of a heavy rain." 42 So Ahab went off to eat and drink, but Elijah climbed to the top of Carmel, bent down to the ground and put his face between his knees. 43 "Go and look toward the sea," he told his servant. And he went up and looked. "There is nothing there," he said. Seven times Elijah said, "Go back." 44 The seventh time the servant reported, "A cloud as small as a man's hand is rising from the sea." So, Elijah said, "Go and tell Ahab, 'Hitch up your chariot and go down before the rain stops you." 45 Meanwhile, the sky grew black with clouds, the wind rose, a heavy rain came on and Ahab rode off to Jezreel.*

New Orleans, and most of Louisiana were only part of the disaster. Mississippi, Alabama and parts of other states, including small cities and communities were devastated. 70,000 homes, 120,000 people, schools, businesses, stores and churches were polluted, with a mix of crude oil and mud sludge a foot deep in the streets, and carried up into all of the buildings. The EPA said there was no way to clean the pollution. Entire cities would have to be bulldozed. About 80 United Methodist pastors in South Louisiana said their congregations were scattered and buildings gone or unusable. There were no funds, no place, and no people for them to perform the ministry which they vowed to perform. Multiply this times all of the other denominations. Crops were ruined, farm buildings destroyed or unusable, farm equipment ruined, and soil polluted with salt water and crude oil. The fishing industry, shipbuilding, and tourism, would be gone for a good while.

What can I do? I can pray, volunteer, and support whatever my church and other Christian relief organizations choose to do for flood survivors. This is what Christians do.

"Father, guide me to the place where I can be the best help and comfort to those who are stricken. Amen"

Avoid Burn-out

There was an episode on the Twilight Zone of a businessman, burned out, and exhausted from the day, who went to sleep on the train. He dreamed of a place where workdays had no deadlines, and no competition to keep his job. Life was more than just coming home to sleep, and returning the next day to a job he hated. The conductor gently shook him. "This is Willoughby sir, your stop." He had gone to sleep and woke in the 19th century. He stepped off the train onto a wooden platform with hand baggage carts, at a station bearing a sign that said "Willoughby." Beyond the station were dirt streets. People were traveling on foot, by horse back, and in buggies. Beyond was a park, where couples walked the paths, children were playing, and a band was tuning up in the gazebo.

My childhood was much like Willoughby. We lived three miles from town, and if the weather was fit, and some times when it wasn't, I walked to school. On the way home I passed the Allis Chalmers tractor dealer where I stopped to look at the new bright orange tractors. Another block down was the town library, good for an occasional stop, then the drug store for a coke, if I had a few cents, then to the Chevy dealer to see the new models, and then home. I seldom walked far. Someone would always pick me up.

No one had house keys, we played scrub softball and tag. No one ever won. We just played. On Sunday, we went to church and families took turns having the preacher home for dinner. No merchants were open on Sunday. It was reserved for rest, family picnics, reunions and visiting relatives.

Would you like to find Willoughby?

In Matthew 11 Jesus said, *"Come to me, all you who are struggling hard and carrying heavy loads, and I will give you rest. Put on my yoke, and learn from me. I'm gentle and humble. And you will find rest for yourselves. My yoke is easy to bear, and my burden is light."*

"Lord help us follow Christ, not worldly things." AMEN

And the Rain Came Down

A man built a house just above the flood plain of a great river. One night he went to bed during a heavy rainstorm and when he woke the river had swollen beyond its normal flood level. Water was in his house and rising. It was too late to get out so he crawled into the attic and broke a hole through the roof. He held on to his fireplace chimney and before long a boat came along offering him a ride to safety, but he declined. He had prayed for God to save him, so they could go on and save others and he would wait on God. As the water crept up the chimney a helicopter came offering him a ride, but he declined with the same explanation. The water rose still higher and the man drowned. When he reached heaven, he complained to St. Peter that his prayer had not been answered, but St. Peter said, "I don't understand. We sent a boat and a helicopter."

Almost everyone in the church knew that I was having knee surgery, and many prayers went up on my behalf, for which I am very grateful. My point is, "What happens when prayers go up? God covered me with a good Christian surgeon, nurses, and anesthesiologist. I was in a faith-based hospital and the nurses and staff were a blessing to me. Did God have a hand in my healing? You betcha. Not only did his hand mend me, but he also sent people to take care for me both physically and spiritually.

Our best prayers are those for and from others, and we don't question God's methods or reasons.

In James 5:15 we read, *"Prayer that comes from faith will heal the sick, for the Lord will restore them to health. And if they have sinned, they will be forgiven."*

"Thank you for the prayers of Christian friends Lord, and forgive me of my sins." AMEN

When I was a Child

The little boy next door had his bike tied in a tree with one rope on the back of his seat and another to the handlebars. A stepladder was placed where he could climb up and sit on the bike, looking like the kids in E.T. and pedaling across the sky, getting nowhere, and a little dangerous, but, to him it was his fantasy world, lost in dreams, choosing his own destiny. As a child, our summer playground was a hedgerow of Chinaberry trees between a pasture and a cotton field. We had forts, dugouts, and tree houses scattered all through the long row of trees. Our weapon was the slingshot; not the Y shaped kind, but a long strip of inner tube tied to an old shoe tongue. A Chinaberry could leave a whelp, but fortunately twelve-year-old moving targets weren't easy to hit. There were two good things about our wars. Neither side ever won or lost and everyone went home for dinner.

Being happy and content, whatever the circumstances, was dreaming, using my imagination, and listening to Grandmother as she told us Bible stories. I stood beside the Jordan and watched John baptize Jesus, I sat on the ground on the side of a mountain and listened to the Sermon on the Mount, and entered the big gates and stood in the courtyard of the temple.

Contentment as a child is making the most of what we have. If I watch the children as they play, and remember my youth, perhaps I can better understand Paul's letter when he wrote to the Philippians.

Philippians. 4:11-13. *"I am not saying this because I am in need, for I have learned to be content whatever the circumstances. I know what it is to be in need, and I know what it is to have plenty. I have learned the secret of being content in any and every situation, whether well fed or hungry, whether living in plenty or in want. I can do everything through him who gives me strength."*

"Lord give me the ability to be content with what I have. AMEN,"

Toot-Toot

When I was 13, I was in the 8th grade. My school had four-rooms on a gravel road and the parking lot doubled as a playground. Everyone rode the bus, save two girls. Their father owned a Chrysler dealership and drove a big baby blue Chrysler New Yorker convertible, with big chrome air horns on huge front fenders. Every day he picked his girls up after school and much to their embarrassment announced his arrival with a big WHAA-WHAA. There can be many horns in a band, like the sweet sound of the flute, the trumpet reaching for the sky, the trombone, the mellow sound of the sax, and twice I have heard huge bass trombones that can blow you out of the water. The horns in a band can make a wondrous sound in concert, under the direction of a leader, blending their parts. Yes, a band, can make a grand sound. But all of the members have to play their part so they will blend.

Voices are our own horns. When I was teaching, my teacher's voice could make Johnny in the back of the room hear me with no problem over a class of noisy teens. The song goes, "Daddy sang bass, Mama sang tenor." We all have different voices, some high and some low. Some loud and some soft. There are voices that can pierce sheet steel and some so gentle they can only be heard in the calm. Some sound like thunder. One person can have many voices. A mother's voice can calm a crying baby or pronounce doom and destruction for Mary Sue if she doesn't clear the table and wash the dishes.

The day WWII ended I was at my grandfather's office. Horns were blowing everywhere. We walked outside and all we could hear was LOUD shouting, "The war is over." It was beautiful.

How magnificent we are as a church, with each of us as a part of the body, as "We make disciples of Jesus Christ."
I Corinthians 12:12 *"The body is a unit, though it is made up of many parts; and though all its parts are many, they form one body."*

"Dear Lord, direct us to do your work in concert. AMEN"

<h1 style="text-align:center">For the Love of Children</h1>

I was sitting in our son and daughter-in-law's living room one day when our youngest granddaughter was about a year and a half. She held a small stuffed animal in her hands and was alternately walking and running around the sofa. Every few trips she would stop, get up in my lap, and give me a hug. Then she would get down and repeat her around and around trips. Now she is two and a half. Last evening, she was at our house for dinner. She was sitting next to me on a stool and stopped, her spoon in midair, to tell me Grandma made good soup.

Totally out of the blue one day our oldest granddaughter asked me what "I love you" meant. I told her it meant that you were very special to me and I liked you a whole lot. After thinking for a few minutes, she said, "Grandpa I love you."

A friend's wife had been taking a neighbor's small son to Vacation Bible School every day. He had made very little comment about his class. One evening, his mother overheard him singing in the bathtub, "Jesus loves me, I know this".

When our pastor's daughter was about three, she invited one of her friends to church. That family is now part of the church.

The Upper Room once told the story of a five-year-old who asked her daddy if he would send her to her room when she was having a bad day. She said, "I can scream and yell till the hurt and pain is gone and then Jesus can fill the empty place.

Mark 10:15-16 *[15] I assure you that whoever doesn't welcome God's kingdom like a child will never enter it." [16] Then he hugged the children and blessed them.*

"Father, make us like children, that we may enter your kingdom." AMEN

It Ain't no Whistle Stop

As we boarded the train in Mineola I thought "It's really great that a small town like Mineola was able to save the town as a regular train stop." We were on our way to a five-day vacation in San Antonio, and getting there was half the fun. I sat by the window, listening to the clickety clack, watching big clouds, and seeing the rolling hills and plains of Texas. I was in my boyhood. Trees, pastures, cotton fields, corn and maze slid by. I even enjoyed the back streets of the little towns. About half way, I went down to the concession bar for a cup of coffee. I chatted with the man working the concession, and learned his home was in St. Louis. He works five days on and five days off on the "road" from Chicago to San Antonio, and has worked the railroad for 27 years and plans to work a while longer. "Where are you from sir?" He said.

"Just a whistle stop," I told him. "Mineola."

"Mr." he said, "Mineola ain't no whistle stop. If it weren't for that town, for one lady who went to Washington, no one on the Chicago-San Antonio run would have a job. They were the only town that went to bat for us. They saved the whole run. Service from Chicago to San Antonio was about to be terminated. No sir! Mineola ain't no whistle stop. They get first class service." The train was on the second track when we returned Mineola, but two engines and ten coaches switched so that two passengers needn't walk to the station platform. That's 1st class service.

The Jews were overwhelmed and gave up. They didn't think the Temple was worth the energy to rebuild. They didn't need it.
Ezra thought it was, and in Ezra 3:12 we find these words.
"But many of the older priests and Levites and family heads, who had seen the former temple, wept aloud when they saw the foundation of this temple being laid, while many others shouted for joy."

Jesus thought the church wasn't no whistle stop. He loved us enough that He died for it, and that is first class service.

"Thank you, Jesus, for giving your life and love for us." AMEN

Let Us Pray

"Listening prayers" are difficult, but may possibly be the most productive. The tweeting of a bird, a squirrel scolding a cat as it circles its tree, the sound of joyous laughter, a beautiful sunset, or the moon glistening on a lake are some of the fun things God says to us. But really listening to what God is saying is a tough thing to do. It takes a lot of listening. In the book, "Joshua and The Shepherd," David Campbell is greatly concerned about the Church. He says, "I spent the entire night in prayer, not talking, just listening. It was terrifying." Listening prayers are difficult.

Mature Christians, don't pray for a new ball, or a lot of money, but, how much prayer time is spent asking God for the things we want that we could get ourselves? Whatever we beg of God, let us also work for it instead of looking for spiritual favors, and relying on God for those things we are capable of doing for ourselves. Prayer should not be giving God reasons why he should grant this, or reasons why what we want is good for us. Prayer is not just asking. It's a reverent petition made to God, an act of communion with him, an object of worship, such as in devotion, confession, praise, or thanksgiving. Prayer is not idle wishing or for amusement. It is the most potent instrument of action. It is better in prayer to have a heart without words than words without a heart. We give thanks for what we have and what we have been given. It is good that we pray for the needs of the Church, for others, and that we pray paying attention to something or someone other than self.

In Mark 11:24 Jesus says, *"Therefore I say unto you, what things soever ye desire, when ye pray, believe that ye receive them, and ye shall have them."*

Set aside fifteen minutes a day, and spend half talking and half listening, and if you need a starting place, just start out like Jesus taught us.

"Our Father which art in Heaven." And end with, "AMEN"

The Hurrier I Go the Behinder I Get

One of my favorite sayings is, "The hurrier I go the behinder I get." Those may not be real words but they do portray the results of untested short cuts or too much speed. Once when I was in my teens I was moving our hay bailer from one farm to another. There was a little valley with a high water crossing at the bottom. That's a concrete slab section instead of a bridge, where water flows across in wet weather. My tractor would run about 18 M.P.H. at top speed and the bailer weighed two or three times the weight of the tractor. I decided to make a little time by shifting to neutral and coasting down the hill. Tractor brakes aren't much, even dangerous at high speeds, and there was no way to get the tractor back in gear. The front of the tractor was bouncing, the wind was whistling through my hair, and all I could do was hold a straight line as best I could. I didn't even have time to pray, just say, "Thank you Lord," when I finally rolled to a stop. For a while I thought my children would lose their father before I even met their mother.

Sooner or later we learn that the hurrier we go the behinder we get. The scripture tells us there is only one way.

Proverbs 21:5 says, *"The plans of the diligent end up in profit, but those who hurry end up with loss."*

John 14:5-6 *⁵Thomas said to him, "Lord, we don't know where you are going, so how can we know the way?" ⁶Jesus answered, "I am the way and the truth and the life. No one comes to the Father except through me.*

There is only one way, with no short cuts. Jesus said so.

"Lord, show me the way that I might not stumble." AMEN

Propped Up with a Post

Have you ever seen an old building propped up? I haven't for a long time, but I remember seeing many of them when I was younger. Picture an old un-painted farm building. As time goes by, the wood dries and shrinks, some joints decay and loosen and if the structure wasn't built with braces in its frame it will start leaning away from the prevailing winds. To save old buildings farmers sometimes put support poles against the side opposite the wind, kind of like putting your shoulder into pushing a load. You can also find props against fence posts, trees, anything that is leaning over and in jeopardy of falling. If flood water comes against a fence, debris will build until pressure from the water makes the fence lean. Cattle rubbing against old buildings, fences and even small trees make them lean. When you drive an old road through the countryside keep your eyes peeled for propping posts.

My grandfather had an old corncrib that was propped. I got to thinking about it, and how much I was like that old corncrib. I've been around now for 83 years, a long time. I've withstood a lot of life's storms and bad weather in life, but I'm still standing. However, I find myself leaning to one side from time to time, so I like to ask the Lord to prop me up on the side that's leaning with the wind, because I get to leaning away from doing His work, leaning from anger, bitterness, and a lot of things that I shouldn't.

From time to time all of us need support. In 2 Kings Naaman, commander of the army of the king of Aram, said to the prophet Elisha,

2 Kings 5:18-19 *May the* LORD *forgive your servant for this one thing: When my master enters the temple to bow down and he is leaning on my arm and I have to bow there also—when I bow down in the temple, may the* LORD *forgive your servant for this."*
19 "Go in peace," Elisha said."

If you need some support, most churches have extra prop poles, and they're open to sharing.

"Lord, prop me up, so I'll stand straight and tall again, to glorify You." AMEN

I Have Favorites

What is my favorite car? I prefer American made, but, after having taught auto-mechanics for 45 years, and driven many makes and models, there isn't a particular one I prefer over another. If they are well maintained most of today's cars will give years of service. Perhaps the most confusing is what determines American and foreign made? Parts are made all over the world. China makes a lot of electronic parts, Germany makes engines and Daimler purchased Chrysler. Our last family car was a Buick made in Mexico, my work car is a Nissan pick-up made in Smyrna, Tennessee, and Toyota has a large factory in California. Go figure. What is my favorite car? One that is paid for.

What is my favorite bible verse? Here are some of the answers I received to the question when I asked it of my Sunday school class.

Psalms 46:1 *"God is our refuge and strength, a very present help in trouble.* "Psalms 23:1 *"The LORD is my shepherd; I shall not want,"*

The entire 23rd Psalm, and the entire chapter of 1 Corinthians 13.

When I was a boy we quoted bible verses while standing in a circle. If you couldn't think of one you had to sit down. The last one standing was the winner. One of the favorite verses was from the story of Lazarus, found in John 11:35. The shortest verse in the Bible. *"Jesus wept."*
Probably the all-time favorite is John 3:16. *"For God so loved the world that he gave his only Son, so that everyone who believes in him may not perish but have eternal life."*

What is your favorite verse, or favorite thing? Think about this. What would it be like to get a smile and a hug from Jesus? Or maybe this prayer?

"Thank you, O Lord, for the gift of Your son Jesus. AMEN"

Tools of a Layman

A Big Chief notebook and a number 2 pencil were my main tools when I was a schoolboy. I learned how to add and subtract, memorized my multiplication tables and learned long division. Now, a calculator, I pad, computer, and many other electronic gadgets have taken over our lives. If I want to read, all I need is one of those new electronic books and I can load it with hundreds, maybe even thousands of books. But, one of the things not changed is the contents of the Bible and even then, I can use the Bible on my computer to find, copy and paste any reference from dozens of translations. I can also quote John Wesley, The Interpreter's Bible Commentary or any one of several other commentaries. A couple of clicks and I am on the internet reading about the history of the Jews, the geography of Canaan that Moses saw from atop Mt. Nebo or first century life in Rome. I was a teacher for 45 years and have a lot of experience. Now that doesn't mean I am a great teacher but it does mean that I have the personal tools, know how to use them, and am faced with an awesome responsibility.

These words from Luke 12:48 (NKJV). *"For everyone to whom much is given, from him much will be required; and to whom much has been committed, of him they will ask more."*

Even those who have never been professional teachers can easily, with a little practice and time, prepare and present a descent lesson from our Sunday school and Bible study material.

If you are holding a job that feeds and clothes a family, you must have some talent for doing something. Even our hobbies develop skills. If God has given us these talents, then He has also given us the responsibility of developing them, using them for good.

"Lord, you have given me tools; the tools to do Your work. Guide my hands as I hone my skills to do the work that the Lord Jesus left for me to do." AMEN

Talents

As I sat at my desk where I volunteer in the surgery waiting room, I watched Sarah, about three years old, sitting in the middle of the main isle. She very carefully tied her shoes, looked at them, and then untied them and started over. She had just learned how and was having fun practicing. I had noticed a blond headed boy and his sister, in their mid-teens, sitting together in the waiting room. They had to be brother and sister, same blond hair, blue eyes and the same features. A little later the boy came into our refreshment room and fixed two cups of hot chocolate. I jokingly said, "You must be thirsty." He said, "One is for my sister." A little later the girl came in and got two donuts. She looked at me and said, "One is for my brother." I asked her which of them was the older. "She said, "He is. By about five minutes." A little later I noticed the early hour had caught up with them. She had gone to sleep with her head on his shoulder and he was asleep with his head tilted over on top of hers. All three of these children were practicing, tying shoes, being kind, and loving one another. God gives us all sorts of talents and almost daily we observe new tools and ways for using them. To deny them is to deny what God has given us responsibility over.

Even sharing our thoughts in a Sunday school class is a talent worth sharing. We learn these things from Jesus' teaching, from examples in the scripture and from one another.

Paul said to the Philippians: *8 From now on, brothers and sisters, if anything is excellent and if anything is admirable, focus your thoughts on these things: all that is true, all that is holy, all that is just, all that is pure, all that is lovely, and all that is worthy of praise. 9 Practice these things: whatever you learned, received, heard, or saw in us. The God of peace will be with you.*

"Lord teach us the use of the talents we have learned through the study of your word. AMEN"

Be a Sculpture

When old people were little boys and girls, Ivory soap proclaimed, "99 and 44/100% pure and it floats." It was good for laundry, washing dishes, taking baths, and an un-advertised use as a carving medium. Teachers had students carve statues and other art from Ivory soap bars. But I think that art form has been lost.

When our son was a cub scout, he made a Pine Wood Derby race car. The kit had a block of pine wood, 4 plastic wheels and nails for axles. He carved the body, put the wheels on it, but it seemed rather light for a gravity-powered racer. So, we weighted the bottom with lead to bring it up to the maximum allowable weight. He won first in den and first in pack that year, and first in den and third in pack the other. We had fun but the most memorable incident was a little boy with a rather shabby racer. He had no help in building it and no parent came to the event with him. There were only two un-raced cars left in his den, and his car was beaten badly, but he was awarded a little trophy for finishing second in a two-car race. No one was there to share his victory but he proudly showed the trophy to anyone who would look. He had done his best and I felt more than obligated to praise him for his achievement.

Imagine Jesus as a small boy in his father's carpenter shop, picking up scraps of wood and building things. Of course, He became the master whittler with the ability to take a broken soul and with grace, love and kindness carve a kind and loving being.

Try carving out some new friends with tools of love and kindness. You'll make some beautiful ones.

Matthew 21:42, *Jesus said, "Haven't you ever read in the scriptures, the stone that the builders rejected has become the cornerstone. The Lord has done this, and it's amazing in our eyes?*

"Thank you Lord for building us in your image. AMEN"

Angel or Friend

I've quoted my grandmother so much. At 85 her mind was clear as a crystal but then she fell and broke her hip. At first her mind was still good, but then she began to get confused. Toward the end, she thought I was my grandfather or an uncle. She needed an angel to look over her but I was young and unsure of what to do. I think I comforted her but I felt inadequate, certainly not an angel.

Would you like to be an angel? All of us want to be angels someday. But I'm talking about the right now. Angels do exist, although they don't have wings. They are sometimes called friends. Some are even strangers and sometimes we can become one.

Hebrews. 13: [2] *Forget not to show love unto strangers: for thereby some have entertained angels unawares.*

As for friends, would you rather have a friend or be one. Jesus calls his followers "friends" and also to be friends.

In John 15 he says, *"*[12] *This is my commandment, that ye love one another, even as I have loved you.* [13] *Greater love hath no man than this, that a man lay down his life for his friends.* [14] *Ye are my friends, if ye do the things which I command you.* [15] *No longer do I call you servants; for the servant knoweth not what his lord doeth: but I have called you friends; for all things that I heard from my Father, I have made known unto you.*

I received this poem a from a friend, while I struggling with a loved one with dementia.

Don't ask me to remember, or try to make me understand.
Let me rest, know you're with me, kiss my cheek, hold my hand.
I'm confused beyond your concept. I am sad and sick and lost.
All I know is that I need you, to be with me, at all cost.
Do not lose your patience with me, do not scold or curse or cry.
I can't help the way I'm acting, can't be different 'though I try.
Just remember that I need you, cause' the best of me is gone.
Please don't fail to stand beside me, love me 'till my life is done.
"Thank you, God, for the gifts of love and friendship, AMEN."

Memories

Hello friend! How is your memory? Who is the Lt. Governor of your state, the wealthiest person in the world, Miss America, Country music's top male vocalist of the year, and who won last year's Super Bowl? How did you do? I failed miserably. We don't remember the headlines of yesterday. They were the best, but when the cheering died, they were forgotten.

Now put a name with your favorite school teacher, a friend who helped you through a difficult time, one who made you feel special, and three friends you enjoy spending time with. You don't have to see or be with friends every day. Years can go by and you don't have to give up a friend to gain another. Friends make a difference in life, not because they have the most credentials, the most money, or the most awards. You can't make a few clicks on Facebook and gain a new best friend. Best friends are people who are caring, kind, loving and genuinely care about you.

There were teachers I wouldn't have thought of as friends at the time, but they were. I've had neighbors who were real friends. Probably my best and really good friends are fellow church members. There have been people whom I have met along the way who befriended me but whose names I never knew. I got to know my current best friend when I preached his father's funeral while our pastor was on vacation.

Lastly, a best friend is someone whom we can trust with our deepest thoughts without fear. Even Jesus showed trust in a friend from the cross:

John 19:26-27 "When Jesus saw his mother and the disciple whom he loved standing beside her, he said to his mother, "Woman, here is your son." Then he said to the disciple, "Here is your mother." And from that hour the disciple took her into his own home.

"Thank you Lord for friends. AMEN."

Oh yes! Lest I forget. In order to have a friend you have to be one.

Using Our Senses

How often do we take for granted, what we can see, hear, smell and observe in so many ways?

John the Baptist sent some of his disciples to see if Jesus was the messiah.

Luke 7:21-23 [21] *Right then, Jesus healed many of their diseases, illnesses, and evil spirits, and he gave sight to a number of blind people.* [22] *Then he replied to John's disciples, "Go, report to John what you have seen and heard. Those who were blind are able to see. Those who were crippled now walk. People with skin diseases are cleansed. Those who were deaf now hear. Those who were dead are raised up. And good news is preached to the poor"*

In Luke 8, He (Jesus) spoke by a parable: [5] *"A sower went out to sow his seed. And as he sowed, some fell by the wayside; and it was trampled down, and the birds of the air devoured it.* [6] *Some fell on rock; and as soon as it sprang up, it withered away because it lacked moisture.* [7] *And some fell among thorns, and the thorns sprang up with it and choked it.* [8] *But others fell on good ground, sprang up, and yielded a crop a hundredfold." When He had said these things He cried, "He who has ears to hear, let him hear!"* [9] *Then His disciples asked Him, saying, "What does this parable mean?"* [10] *And He said, "To you it has been given to know the mysteries of the kingdom of God, but to the rest it is given in parables, that 'Seeing they may not see, And, hearing they may not understand.'*

If we use our eyes and ears as we live daily in God's world, and study His word, it will be revealed to us. Sunday school is such an important part of our church life; a place where we see and hear and join together in learning the teachings of the scripture.

"Lord open our senses that we might see, hear, smell, and feel Your world around us. AMEN."

Do What You Were Meant to Do

Rusty the dog died of cancer, so we no longer have a little dog in and out of the house all the time. I miss him following me around all day when I am outside working. One of our neighbors has a little dog, a Shih Tzu, which is about seven or eight pounds of white fluff on four short legs. I think his family would like for him to be a sweet, prissy little lap dog and he probably is, at home, but when they let him out to play, he comes to our house and becomes the great hunter, a squirrel dog. When he spots a squirrel, he breaks into a dead run to catch it. Of course, his dead run is a gentle stride for the squirrel who sees him coming, lopes over to the nearest tree and climbs just high enough to aggravate him. He lies down facing the tree, head thrown back, barking and swishing his little flag of a tail. I don't know how he thinks he will get the squirrel down but I have seen him lie there for up to an hour before giving up to go on safari for more adventure.

Perhaps we should go out to play, hunt our squirrels and go on safari. Our natural instincts coupled with our knowledge of God's word would lead us to some great hunting days. John Wesley once said, "Give me one hundred preachers who fear nothing but sin, and desire nothing but God, and I care not a straw whether they be clergymen or laymen. Such alone will shake the gates of hell and set up the kingdom of heaven on earth." That would be a good safari for any Christian.

The little dog doesn't know what to do once the squirrel is up the tree, so he barks. However, Christ has told us what to do. He told his disciples in Matthew 7 to ask, seek, and knock. He has equipped us to seek God, to go out and hunt and find our squirrel.

Matthew 7:7 *"Ask and it will be given to you; seek and you will find; knock and the door will be opened to you."*
If I don't know what else to do I can always pray, be kind to someone, smile, and if just one person says to me, "You've made my day," that makes my day.

"Lord, instill in me the desire to seek others for you. AMEN"

The Beauty of Nature

Bluebirds are territorial little creatures. A few days ago, we were sitting on the patio and I noticed a pair of bluebirds fluttering around our bluebird house. More bluebirds began flying around and I could see them collecting in the trees. At one point, I counted 12 birds in a group and could still see many more flying from tree to tree. This seemed unusual for birds that are normally so territorial. They were evidently gathering for their winter migration. The next day they were all gone.

One of the differences between the birds and us is that we worry and fret over so many other things than guarding our nest. We worry about what we eat, what we wear, what kind of a car we drive and what position we have in the community.

In Matthew 6 Jesus said: *[19] "Do not store up for yourselves treasures on earth, where moth and rust consume and where thieves break in and steal; [20] but store up for yourselves treasures in heaven, where neither moth nor rust consumes and where thieves do not break in and steal. [21] For where your treasure is, there your heart will be also."*

In verse *[26] Look at the birds of the air, for they neither sow nor reap nor gather into barns; yet your heavenly Father feeds them. Are you not of more value than they? And in verse [30] Now if God so clothes the grass of the field, which today is here, and tomorrow is thrown into the oven, will He not much more clothe you, O you of little faith?"*

Our late summer is over. The temperature has dropped and acorns are falling like rain. Jesus walked everywhere he went. He must have been very much in touch with grass along the path, wild flowers in the fields, rocks, steep places and birds of the air. He didn't worry about whether or not there was enough savings to pay for his retirement home or if his house needed painting or a million other of the worries of today. He was content with what he had and so too should we.

"Thank you Lord for the gifts of your creation." AMEN

Beauty of Spring – Newness of Life

The days are getting longer and the temperature is slowly rising. In fact, I have noticed my energy level is rising. It's been a couple of weeks since I've seen a big flock of Blackbirds, but early in the morning bird songs fill the air and the squirrels are playing everywhere. An Armadillo is trying to make his home under my little shop and Rusty, the dog, has been lying in the sun on the little rise above the garage. The Tulip tree, Forsythia and Daffodil blooms have come and gone. Dogwoods, Azaleas, Tulips and a few other spring bloomers are lighting up the landscape as the grass and trees turn green. Last year's gangly little girls are looking like young women and the boys who thought girls were yucky last year are starting to look at them with a new eye. Spring is in the air.

Was the Garden of Eden like that? Who in the world could blow a deal like that? Maybe that's where the old adage started, "The grass is always greener on the other side of the fence."

God gives the children of Israel final advice as they enter the promised land. Deut.[11:11-15] *"But the land you are crossing the Jordan to take possession of is a land of mountains and valleys that drinks rain from heaven. It is a land the LORD your God cares for; the eyes of the LORD your God are continually on it from the beginning of the year to its end. So, if you faithfully obey the commands I am giving you today~to love the LORD your God and to serve him with all your heart and with all your soul~then I will send rain on your land in its season, both autumn and spring rains, so that you may gather in your grain, new wine and oil. I will provide grass in the fields for your cattle, and you will eat and be satisfied."*

Easter. Our promise of spring. After being crucified Jesus, rose on the third day to live again, promising us the same new life. Believe in him, be faithful and do the work he has left for us and we shall surely see the new spring, one that will last forever.

"Thank you, O God, AMEN.?

God is the Weather Man

It's raining today. It rained yesterday and the day before and the day before that. The rain is coming mostly in the form of a drizzle with occasional heavy spells. In all, it is just enough to keep me from working in the yard and doing outdoor things I would much rather be doing. In fact, if I had my druthers, the rain would stop and come back in July and August when we really need it, but, I'm not running the weather. That's God's job. Fifteen places in the New Testament alone mention rain.

Acts 14:17 *"He has blessed you by giving you rain from above as well as seasonal harvests and satisfying you with food and happiness."*
James 5:7b *"Consider the farmer who waits patiently for the coming of rain in the fall and spring, looking forward to the precious fruit of the earth."*

These quotations point to the seasons, the sun and rain and all those things we call Mother Nature are under God's control. He established them and set them free to provide life over all the earth. In the first chapter of Genesis, God spoke to man and said:

"Be fertile and multiply; fill the earth and master it. Take charge of the fish of the sea, the birds in the sky, and everything crawling on the ground." 29 Then God said, "I now give to you all the plants on the earth that yield seeds and all the trees whose fruit produces its seeds within it. These will be your food. 30 To all wildlife, to all the birds in the sky, and to everything crawling on the ground—to everything that breathes—I give all the green grasses for food." And that's what happened. 31 God saw everything He had made: it was supremely good.

And so, it was and still is that God put us in charge of His creation. He gave us, enough sense to fertilize and water when it is needed and not to misuse or abuse that which we are responsible for, and this is why we continue to give Him thanks for all over which we have stewardship to care for and use as we need.

At meal time, or bedtime, or whenever we think of it, don't forget to say;

"Lord thank you for all of your creation and your son Jesus Christ."
AMEN

Blessed Are The Peacemakers

This story is found in the writings of Theodoret, Bishop of Cyrrhus in Syria. It can be found in Book V, Chapter XXVI: Of Honorius, the Emperor and Telemachus the monk.

"Emperor Honorius," who inherited the empire of Europe, put a stop to the gladiatorial held at Rome. A monk, named Telemachus took on a simple, peaceful, way of life. A voice told him to go to Rome without knowing why and follow the crowds to the Coliseum where two gladiators were fighting. He tried to get between them to stop them, shouting three times, "In the name of Christ, forbear!" endeavoring to stop the men who were wielding their weapons against one another. The spectators of the slaughter were indignant, and inspired by the triad fury of the demon who delights in those bloody deeds, stoned the peacemaker. The Christian Emperor Honorius, however, was impressed. It spurred him to issue a historic ban on gladiator fights. The last known fight in Rome was on 1 January 404 AD, given as the date of Telemachus' martyrdom.

President Ronald Reagan told the story of "the little monk" (at the Annual National Prayer Breakfast on February 2, 1984). Unfortunately, there may be a couple of mistakes in the story that are usually perpetuated, whenever it is told. One is an argument over the exact date, the other over whether the crowd stoned him or a gladiator ran him through with a sword. The second is the most credible.

Matthew 5:9 – *"Blessed are the peacemakers: for they shall be called the children of God."*

Not all Christians are called to full-time Christian Ministry, nor are we all required to give up our life, but we are all called by God to share our faith (witness) with those who are not Christians.

In one way or the other the members of all Christian Churches are charged with sharing our witness.

Jesus said: Mark 16:15, *"Go into the whole world and proclaim the good news to every creature."*

"Lord, give us the courage to stand up for our faith, as did Jesus."

AMEN

Testing

When Annie was a little girl she had a nurse's outfit for her Barbie doll. She wanted to be a nurse when she grew up. Now she had completed four years of nursing school and had two years of experience. She wanted to be a surgical nurse but nothing had opened for her. She had become friends with one of the surgeons whose advice was to just hang in there, an opportunity would come.

One day he met her in the hall and said, "Annie, I have made arrangements for you to try out as a surgical nurse. Be in the surgery scrub room at seven in the morning ready to join me in surgery."

She was so excited she couldn't sleep that night, but early in the morning she was ready to go. Her job was to keep track of his surgical tools and when he finished, he said, "I'm going to close."

Annie said, "You can't close yet doctor. One of the sponges is missing. We had twelve and there are only eleven here."

The doctor said, "That will be okay. It will show up."

Annie said, "But doctor! You can't close. What if it's inside the patient?"

The Doctor said, "I am the doctor and I'm going to close."

Her face was red. Brand new in surgery and contradicting the doctor would be the end of her dream job but she had to make one more try and said, "Doctor, you put me in charge of keeping track of your surgical tools and we're one sponge short." Red faced, and out of breath, she waited.

The doctor laughed as he moved his foot to show the sponge he had been standing on and said, "You'll be OK." It had been a test.

God gives us tests from time to time. Whenever it happens, your conscience will let you know it's time to stick out your neck and stand between right and wrong. And, no matter what happens to you, God will laugh and say, "You'll be OK."

Psalm 26:2 *"Examine me, Lord; put me to the test! Purify my mind and my heart. Amen"*

Keep Warm

Jon was just a good man. If you needed help Jon was there. His wife and three children attended the local church, and on Sunday evenings he took his two oldest children to their youth meeting and picked them up afterward. He took the youngest to VBS in early summer and built his wife's women's group a quilting frame, but Jon himself just never got in the habit of attending. He thought church to be a good thing. Friends who attended there were fine people and it was a good influence on his children and in general a good thing for his family, but he just never got in the habit of going.

One Sunday evening in early December his family went to church to plan a Christmas program and before the meeting started the pastor asked Jon's wife how he was doing. She said he was doing fine and when she left he was kicked back in front of a fire with his dog, just relaxing.
The pastor said, "You folks don't need me for this meeting. I think I'll go visiting."

When the pastor knocked on the door Jon answered, invited him in and pulled a second chair over by the fireplace. Both men sat back with the dog between them and watched the fire in silence. After a while the pastor got up, took the tongs from the fireplace, picked up a red- hot coal, placed it on the hearth and sat back down. The red-hot coal cooled down. The pastor picked it up again, nestled it back in the fire among the hot coals, and after a few minutes, it began to glow again. The pastor said he had better get back to church. When Jon opened the door for him he said, "Pastor I really enjoyed our visit and hope you come back. I think the part I appreciated the most was your sermon and I promise I'll be in church Sunday with my family."

Come join us and get warm. The disciples met together to draw on each other's strength.

Acts 2:46 *"Every day, they met together in the temple and ate in their homes. They shared food with gladness and simplicity."*

"Thank you, Lord. for the strength and warmth, we gain from each other. AMEN"

Round and Round, It Goes
And the More It Goes, the Bigger It Grows

A friend asked me, "Why do people join your church and keep coming, willing to support the church and its ministry?"

My answer? "We're friendly, have a lot of love to share, and have a good preacher. Also, our people like each other and want to assimilate anyone who wants to join."

"True," My friend said, "but all churches should be able to say that, and sermons alone don't build and maintain churches. The heart of church growth are its circles, The building and support groups.

The church in Jerusalem heard about the growth of the church in Antioch where they were including everyone, Jews, Gentiles, all that would listen to the word. They sent Barnabas to see what was happening.

Acts 11:23-26 *[23] When he arrived and saw evidence of God's grace, he was overjoyed and encouraged everyone to remain fully committed to the Lord. [24b] A considerable number of people were added to the Lord. [25] Barnabas went to Tarsus in search of Saul. [26] When he found him, he brought him to Antioch. They were there for a whole year, meeting with the church and teaching large numbers of people. It was in Antioch where the disciples were first labeled "Christians."*

The largest and most important group meets for Sunday worship. The strongest? That's the one that meets for fellowship before Sunday school and church and goes out for lunch together after church. Watch them. Each person is anxious to see what the other has done in the last week. It has been seven whole days since they last met and there is a lot of catching up to do. Other circles are men, and women's groups, youth and children's groups, choir, fellowship dinner, Sunday school, prayer groups and even the committees. Circles are what make the church. The more circles you are in the more you are part of it. But, if that is your only circle you really should consider a few more.

He drew a circle that shut me out ~ Heretic, rebel, a thing to flout. But Love and I had the wit to win, we drew a circle that took him in! "Edwin Markham."

"Lord, bless our church that we might grow for you. AMEN"

Fellow Travelers

The other day I was working in my front yard when three young mothers came by on their midmorning walk. One mother was pushing a stroller with an infant, there were two preschool kids, 2 big dogs and a little dust mop of a dog trying to keep up. Every once in a while, they stopped to let the little dog catch up. They were soon past my house, talking and laughing as they went. About fifteen minutes later they came by on the return half of their trip with one mother carrying the infant, the smaller of the two preschoolers riding in the stroller, and the third mother carrying a happy little dust mop of a dog as they continued their journey.

On a good journey, you can smell the roses, watch the sun set, make friends, and enjoy each other's company. In life's journey the big ones help the little ones, the strong help the weak, and the older ones point out things along the way to those who are younger. Each person watches out for the needs of his fellow travelers.

For reasons, I do not understand, strangers traveling together tend to confide things they are not willing to share with friends and family. Even Jesus had strangers who didn't recognize him, share in the loss of the Master on the cross.

Luke 24:13-16 *On that same day, two disciples were traveling to a village called Emmaus, about seven miles from Jerusalem.* [14] *They were talking to each other about everything that had happened.* [15] *While they were discussing these things, Jesus himself arrived and joined them on their journey.* [16] *They were prevented from recognizing him.*

[17] *He said to them, "What are you talking about as you walk along?" They stopped, their faces downcast.* [18] *The one named Cleopas replied, "Are you the only visitor to Jerusalem who is unaware of the things that have taken place there over the last few days?"*

During our walks in life, our little trips, when we are alone, can share with Jesus, confide in him, our greatest, most private needs, and when we are alone with strangers who need to share can offer a friendly ear.

"Thank you Lord for always being with me, no matter where or when I travel, to hear my needs and fears. AMEN"

I Will Change for the Better

Do you remember this popular phrase? "Today is the first day of the rest of your life." The first time I heard it must have been from a motivational speaker in the 60s or 70s. I thought, "What a profound statement. He told people to forget their past and begin a brand new future." However, it wasn't the first-time people would mark a point in their life where they would make permanent change. God made some of the first changes. He moved Adam and Eve out of the garden and told them to do it on their own. He changed Abram's name to Abraham, telling him who he would be, and what he would do. He took Moses off of the sheep ranch and made him a leader of his people. Then he made this new covenant with Abraham in Genesis 17.

Genesis 17:1-5 *Abram was 99 years old, the* LORD *appeared to Abram and said to him, "I am El Shaddai (God Almighty). Walk with me and be trustworthy.* ² *I will make a covenant between us and I will give you many, many descendants."* ³ *Abram fell on his face, and God said to him,* ⁴ *"But me, my covenant is with you; you will be the ancestor of many nations.* ⁵ *And because I have made you the ancestor of many nations, your name will no longer be Abram but Abraham*

God was telling Abraham, "This marks the first day of the rest of your life. Through the many centuries since that time others have had their names changed to mark a new beginning. Jesus changed Simon's name to Peter to become the leader of his church. God changed Saul's name to Paul. His life would be turned around and he would become the missionary to the Gentiles. There have been many others. Another way of marking a new beginning was through baptism. John the Baptist baptized for the remission of sins. "Your sins have been forgiven. Go and sin no more." He also baptized Jesus to mark the beginning of his ministry.

"Forgive us Father of our sins and guide us as we resolve to be improved this next year. AMEN"

People Grumble

During the second world war, Korea, and Vietnam there were A, B, and C food rations. A Rations were the regular meals served in stateside mess halls, B Rations were served where fresh meat and produce were not available, and C Rations were served in the field where cooking was not an option. Monotony became the chief complaint. Sometimes C rations were the only source of food for several weeks, and because of stockpiles, were served as late as 1958 in Vietnam. A and B rations would not have been a choice for Moses and his followers in the wilderness. Quail and Manna would have been it. "We are tired of this food," they said. "We are sick of it." In an episode of MASH the mess sergeant had fixed nothing but canned fish or canned liver for days, and in his outrage Hawkeye said, "I have eaten a river of liver and an ocean of fish."

In Numbers 11 the Israelites wept and said:

[4]"If only we had meat to eat! [5]We remember the fish we used to eat in Egypt for nothing, the cucumbers, the melons, the leeks, the onions, and the garlic; [6]but now our strength is dried up, and there is nothing at all but this manna to look at."..... Moses said, "[13] Where can I get meat for all these people? They keep wailing to me, 'Give us meat to eat!' [14] I cannot carry all these people by myself; the burden is too heavy for me.

Christmas, birthdays, anniversaries, Mother's Day and Father's Day are all times when gifts are given. How often have you received a gift and thought, "That really isn't what I wanted, but even the third blender you received at a bridal shower would probably be accepted graciously.
Is grumbling and complaining ever justified? As they were leaving the chairman's home a lady asked, "How could you have let this happen?" The chairman had no prior knowledge of the problem and couldn't have prevented it, but it was resolved. Then the chairman resigned and he and his family found another church. The lady never knew what she had done.

"Lord teach us to keep our mouths shut and our backs bent in service during times of your servants' hardships. AMEN"

People Rebel

God told Moses to choose a leading man from each of the twelve tribes and send them out as spies to Canaan and see what the land was like, whether the people were strong or weak, whether there were few or many, whether the land was good or bad, and whether the towns they lived in were walled or unfortified. They spied out the land, cut down a branch with a single cluster of grapes that had to be carried on a pole between two men. They also brought some pomegranates and figs and at the end of forty days returned with the fruit, saying the land flowed with milk and honey. Joshua and Caleb said they should go up and occupy it, for they were well able to overcome it, but the other men were afraid, reporting the people to be of great size and living in large cities.

Number 14:1-3 says: *Then all the congregation raised a loud cry, and the people wept that night. ² And all the Israelites complained against Moses and Aaron; the whole congregation said to them, "Would that we had died in the land of Egypt! Or would that we had died in this wilderness! ³ Why is the LORD bringing us into this land to fall by the sword?*

The Israelites believed the worst and would rather follow the ten unfaithful spies. They wanted to go back to Egypt. God would have created a new people under Moses but because of Moses prayer they were saved from destruction. But, none of them were to see the Promised Land. It would be for an unborn generation, all but Joshua and Caleb.

The story brings about many questions; Why did Egypt look better when times were hard? Is it so hard to trust God when we face overwhelming challenges? What does it take to be a Joshua or Caleb? Why were Joshua and Caleb so confident of success? What would we have done, and what would it have been like to have been an Israelite?

"Father, we rebel and refuse to do that which you would have us do. We often do it out of fear, without the faith to follow you. Forgive us Father of our unbelief and strengthen our faith, in Christ's name. AMEN"

Disobeying

Numbers 20:2-4 There was no water for the congregation; so, they gathered together against Moses and against Aaron. ³ The people quarreled with Moses and said, "Would that we had died when our kindred died before the LORD! ⁴ Why have you brought the assembly of the LORD into this wilderness for us and our livestock to die here?

Verses 7-12 ⁷ The LORD spoke to Moses, saying: ⁸ Take the staff, and assemble the congregation, you and your brother Aaron, and command the rock before their eyes to yield its water. ⁹ So Moses took the staff from before the LORD, as he had commanded him. ¹⁰ Moses and Aaron gathered the assembly together before the rock, and he said to them, "Listen, you rebels, shall we bring water for you out of this rock?" ¹¹ Then Moses lifted up his hand and struck the rock twice with his staff; water came out abundantly, and the congregation and their livestock drank. ¹² But the LORD said to Moses and Aaron, "Because you did not trust in me, to show my holiness before the eyes of the Israelites, therefore you shall not bring this assembly into the land that I have given them.

The book of Numbers gives the itinerary of the Israelites as they wander around the desert waiting to die. They didn't know how long it would be, but as we know, it would be 40 years. Moses and Aaron receive the brunt of their grumbling. The people have now reduced their Lord to a killjoy and executioner and turned against Moses. They saw it as Moses' fault for lack of water. God had not asked Moses to perform a miracle for the people to restore faith in he and Aaron and now because of Moses' action they would die in the wilderness with the rest of the people without entering the land of Canaan.

What are the dangers of sin when we accept leadership? How easy is it for our actions to cause others to stumble?

"Lord give me strength and integrity when you call me to do your work." AMEN

Obedience

Obeying God's law and teaching it to our children is more vital than any other lesson, for the church is only one generation away from extinction. We not only teach our children with words but we live by them, making of them examples. John F. Kennedy said, "As we express our gratitude, we must never forget that the highest appreciation is not to just utter words but to live by them." God's law is a gift that keeps on giving and shapes us into the kind of people God can use to change the world.

The first verse of the Shema relates to the kingship of God. "Hear, O Israel: The Lord our God is one Lord. The Shema is more than a prayer. It is a pledge of allegiance, an affirmation of faith with love as the central theme. Love God, neighbor and self. Keep these words, talk about them and fix them in prominent places. Talk about them to your children. The most important place for them is in your heart.

Deuteronomy 6:4-9 [4] *Hear, O Israel: The Lord is our God, the Lord alone.* [5] *You shall love the Lord your God with all your heart, and with all your soul, and with all your might.* [6] *Keep these words that I am commanding you today in your heart.* [7] *Recite them to your children and talk about them when you are at home and when you are away, when you lie down and when you rise.* [8] *Bind them as a sign on your hand, fix them as an emblem on your forehead,* [9] *and write them on the doorposts of your house and on your gates....*

The Shema can be found in 166 places in the NIV. Its most popular quote is from Jesus in Matthew 22:37-40

"Love the Lord your God with all your heart and with all your soul and with all your mind.' [38] *This is the first and greatest commandment.* [39] *And the second is like it: 'Love your neighbor as yourself.'* [40] *All the Law and the Prophets hang on these two commandments."*

We must not only teach with words but we must live by them, making of them examples.

"Lord, who calls us to love you and keep your law, stir in us the desire to learn, serve, and obey your law, as we teach it to others. AMEN"

Trust

A man, picnicking on the beach with his family, went walking. Ahead, he saw what he thought was a stump, but on closer observation it turned out to be a 10-gallon gas can. It had been in the water a long time and was covered with seashells. Now hot and dry, the creatures inside the shells were trying to get out. He tried pulling the can out of the sand but it was buried deep. Then he tried prying the shells off and throwing them back into the sea but they were hard to loosen. His family was now shouting for him to come back. The tide was coming in and it was time to leave. The creatures would not turn loose even to save their own life. He franticly splashed as much water on the container as he could and left, hoping with all his heart that the tide would cover the can before the creatures died. If the shells would turn loose they would survive....

Another man was walking along the sea shore on a beautiful moon lit night. As he walked, the sea shore rose up, way above the water and he could hear the waves crashing on the rocks below. Clouds were starting to cover the sky and the moon was soon blacked out. Although he couldn't see he kept walking, very carefully, but his foot slipped and he tumbled over the edge. As he fell he was grabbing at everything on the cliff front. After he had fallen an eternity, he crashed into some tree branches and was able to grab and hang on. When he stopped bobbing up and down he yelled, "HELP!"

A voice above him calmly said, "You don't need help. Just turn loose.

After a moment of silence, the man said, "Is there anyone else up there?" To which there was no answer.

He held on as long as he could, and when the limb slipped from his grasp, he fell six more inches and landed on the ground.

Try as we may there are some things in which we can only trust the Lord. Even in our worst fears, trust in the Lord will save us.

Proverbs 3:5 *Trust in the Lord with all your heart and lean not on your own understanding;*

"Father, mend our fears and understanding, that we may trust in only You. AMEN"

Strangers

People have a natural desire to find their roots. Most of our ancestors did not marry the one chosen by their parents, or because of their country of origin, race, social status or religion. It was because they were smitten with love, or for convenience, or companionship, a way out of bad circumstances, or a host of other reasons. By whom and from where did we come? Carson is a Scottish name. There are rumors of Jewish blood way back on my mother's side. The real truth of who and where I come from will never be known and doesn't matter. But, God's chosen people seemed for the most part to maintain their bloodline. Abraham was named by God to be the father of a great and numerous people. In the 42 generations of linage from Abraham to Christ were many kings. Heroes like David, wise Solomon, as well as selfish, fearful and inept kings bringing about the captivity in Babylon. There was Ruth; a gentile. In her declaration of love and devotion to her mother-in-law, Naomi, she says in Ruth 1:16

Where you go, I will go, and where you stay I will stay. Your people will be my people and your God my God.

This wasn't a romantic declaration, as some would have it. It was made by a kind and loving person concerned for her widowed mother-in-law who had become bitter because of the loss of her husband and both sons. When Ruth's son was born, the entire community took part in naming him Obed, Father of Jesse and grandfather of King David. There is a lot of history between Abraham and Jesus, the Messiah.

Hebrews 13:2 *Do not forget to show hospitality to strangers, for by so doing some people have shown hospitality to angels without knowing it.*

They were taught to welcome strangers into their midst. Ruth as well as many others were strangers that were welcomed, and played major roles in Hebrew history. So, does the statement

"He came to earth in human form and dwelt among us," mean more to you?

"Thank you Father for sending your son, Jesus, to all of us, AMEN."

God Calls Us

There was a young pastor on a mission trip to Asia. The mission was rewarding but one event was disturbing. Two young college students who were unfamiliar with protestant religion asked him what it was that he did. He explained that he visited people, prayed, led worship, went to the hospital, spent time in counseling and so forth. The more he tried to explain the more difficult it became. Then one of the students had a revelation. "Ah, I think we get it. You are a professional nice guy." It was disconcerting to the young pastor who thought, "Is that all I am?" God uses ordinary people and ordinary things in extraordinary ways.

In Leviticus Chapter 8 are found the "Rites of Ordination." It begins with God speaking to Moses, telling him what to do with Aaron and his sons. He is to take the vestments, anointing oil and unleavened bread and gather all the congregation together. Then he is to say, "This is what the Lord has commanded to be done," and he brought Aaron and his sons forward, and washed them with water.

Leviticus 8:7-9 says, "7 *He put the tunic on him, fastened the sash around him, clothed him with the robe, and put the ephod on him. He then put the decorated band of the ephod around him, tying the ephod to him with it. 8 He placed the breast piece on him, and in the breast piece he put the Urim and the Thummim. 9 And he set the turban on his head, and on the turban, in front, he set the golden ornament, the holy crown, as the Lord commanded Moses.*"

And Moses did all of the things God had told him.

What was so special about an Israelite family, a father and his sons? What was special was God. Clothing is just clothing until God designates it for ministry in his holy place. Bread and grape juice are just bread and grape juice until Jesus commanded we use them in a special way. We are all called at various times in our lives for various services.

"Lord, appoint us and use us in your service as you will, in whatever ways you need us, AMEN."

It is Thine O Lord

It's mine, no it's mine, give it back, you can't have it. Dad taught the kids that it belonged to none of them; it was God's, and then it came back to bite him when a friend wanted to barrow something and he refused. One of the children said, "Dad, that isn't yours—remember?"

Jubilee which happened every fifty years, was a time when all things were restored with God and neighbors. Atonement was when enemies made peace with God and one another for their sins. It was the highest, holiest day of the year, when the high priest offered sacrifices, first for himself and then for the sins of the people and all Israel. Changed to "Reconciliation" in the New Testament, it was a time when the playing field was leveled. What if all of our wealth was gathered and redistributed equally among us? Over time the rich would again get richer and the poor get poorer. Romans 5:10-11 *For if while we were enemies, we were reconciled to God through the death of his Son, much more surely, having been reconciled, will we be saved by his life. [11] But more than that, we even boast in God through our Lord Jesus Christ, through whom we have now received reconciliation.*

Sin separates us from God and neighbor. Even today Atonement, or reconciliation, makes us right with God and is the central doctrine of our faith. Jubilee was about being at one with God, being at one with our neighbor. Do you know what the inscription is on the Liberty Bell?

It is Leviticus 25:10 *"Proclaim liberty throughout all the land unto all the inhabitants thereof."*

Psalm 24:1 we read *"The earth is the Lord's, and everything in it, the world, and all who live in it."*

How do you understand possessions, ownership and stewardship? What is a good steward of the possessions God has entrusted to us?

In Luke 4:18 Jesus said; *"The Spirit of the Lord is on me. He has anointed me to proclaim good news to the poor, sent me to proclaim freedom for the prisoners, recovery of sight for the blind, and to set the oppressed free."*

"Thank you, O Lord, for your bountiful gift of peace and reconciliation. AMEN"

Am I Good?

I don't like myself when I get angry. When I do, I make small minded decisions, behave selfishly, speak out of prejudice, and generally have a bad day. We hear people refer to their saintly grandmother or a particular person who was a pillar in our church who was a saint. All in the past tense because we don't see people becoming saints until after they are deceased. If protestants had saints we would probably have: Dietrich Bonhoeffer, assassinated for resisting Hitler, Clarence Jordan, Founder of Habitat for Humanity, Susana Wesley, Mother of John and Charles Wesley, and E. Stanley Jones, missionary to India. We see saints as perfect people. Any flaws they may have had miraculously evaporated.

We consider holiness with following a very strict moral code of the Christian community, where we have the support of other Christians. It's not the clean, clear air of the Sunday morning golf course, or the soft bank of a lake loaded with bass. Simply observing nature isn't enough.

Peter's commentary on God's call does not ask for unfailing sinlessness but for loving attitudes and actions. John Wesley offered three general rules for being a Christian. "Do no harm, do all the good you can, and Love God." "Thou shall not," is the negative side of our faith. The negative side of the Golden Rule existed long before Jesus. It was said "Do nothing to others you would not have done to you." Do all the good you can. Good deeds reflect holiness but not in a scorekeeping way. Help those we encounter who are in need. Love our neighbor and honor our parents. Love God, attend worship, listen to preaching, pray, and study the scriptures We cannot be holy on our own. We need the community of faith to remind us, to stand beside us, to lift us up when we fall. We sometimes give in to temptation and try to make it on our own. Which raises another question, "Can I be as good a Christian if I only go to church once in a while?" Thus, as Christians we have three general rules. Do no harm, do all the good you can, Love God, and none of these three rules are good without the others.

"Father, help me to love, do no harm, and help Others. AMEN.

Witnessing

A young man had an experience at the Salvation Army Officer's Training School. His assignment was to witness to four people for at least two hrs. His experience was a flop. People didn't care or want to hear what he had to say. As a Christian we each know that we should be witnessing. But, how do you effectively do that?

In Mark 5 Jesus had been on the western side of the Sea of Galilee, where it was predominately Jewish. Then He moved to the eastern side of Galilee, which was mostly gentile. A man was possessed with demons and Jesus drove them into some pigs, which in turn ran over a cliff. The first thing I think after reading this scripture is of a farmer coming to Jesus, wringing his hands, and saying, "Jesus, why did you do that?" Them was my pigs. Now I won't be able to feed my family this winter and I don't even have any breeding stock left. The farmer would have been a gentile, because Jews didn't keep swine. According to Jewish law they were filthy, inedible creatures of no value, but whatever the story, the plight of the pigs is of no concern. The main points are Jesus' control over the demons and the possessed man's response. It was the demons, not the man, who recognized Jesus. They recognized that Jesus was the son of God. The demonic spirits sensed a threat in the presence of divine goodness. In today's world, the man may have been diagnosed with a multi-personality disorder. If that was the case Jesus had the attention of all of those personalities. The man may have had so many problems he didn't know where to start, but in the end Jesus cleansed the man of his multi-problems and left behind a new disciple whom He told to go tell his friends. It appears that the man was so elated he went beyond that.

Psalm 22:22 *I will declare your name to my brothers and sisters; I will praise you in the very center of the congregation!*

Witnessing requires excitement. Are you excited about what God is doing for you?

"Stir in me a new spirit Lord, that makes me want to tell others about You. AMEN"

A Gift from God

Philippians 3:8, 13-16 *I regard everything as loss because of the surpassing value of knowing Christ Jesus my Lord. ¹³ Beloved, I do not consider that I have made it my own; but this one thing I do: forgetting what lies behind and straining forward to what lies ahead, ¹⁴ I press on toward the goal for the prize of the heavenly call of God in Christ Jesus. ¹⁵ Let those of us then who are mature be of the same mind; and if you think differently about anything, this too God will reveal to you. ¹⁶ Only let us hold fast to what we have attained.*

Meb Keflezigi, entered the US from Ethiopia when he was a child, along with his 5 siblings and Christian parents. When he was 12 he ran a 5'20" mile, a remarkable time for a seventh grader. His coach, called the high school coach and said, "I have a future Olympian on my hands" A few years later, Bob Larson, the track, field and cross-country coach at UCLA gave Meb a full scholarship. In 1998 he won four NCAA titles, graduated from UCLA, and became a US citizen all in the same year, and in 04 won the silver medal in Athens with his eye on the gold in the 08 Beijing Olympics.

Then disaster struck in the NY City Marathon. He got a stress fracture in his hip and nearly lost his ability to run, losing a shot at representing the US in the Olympics. In the same race his best friend had a heart attack in the home stretch and fell dead. Then with prayer, rehab, good friends and persistence he came back to run again.

This is what he said: "I was running the New York City Marathon. A race no American had won since Alberto Salazar in 1982. This time I did. Born in a tiny village halfway across the world, I did not make this long journey alone, for I have a mother and father who taught me the power of faith, my education, coaches, and teachers helped me to believe in myself, good friends trained with me, a wife who understands me in a way that goes beyond words and, most of all a God who has boundless love for me. As I passed the spot where my friend Ryan fell, I said a prayer and crossed the finish line first, simply as a child of a loving God.

"Thank you, O God, for your bountiful gifts of life." AMEN

Please Excuse My Broken Key

From som- wh-r- in the back of my m-mory is an analogy of what happ-n-d b-caus- of losing on- hors- sho- nail.

For th- loss of a nail th- sho- was lost; for th loss of th- sho- th- hors- was lost; for th- loss of the hors- th- rid-r was lost; for th loss of th- rid-r th- m-ssag- was lost; for th- loss of th- m-ssag- th- war was lost; and all for th- loss of a nail.

Tak- an old typ-writ-r with on- brok-n k-y. It is old, but works v-ry w-ll, -xc-pt for th- on- k-y. With all th- good k-ys, on- k-y would hardly b- notic-d. But just on- k-y s--ms to ruin th- whol- -ffort.

Hav- you -v-r said to yours-lf, "I'm only on- p-rson. No on- will notic- if I don't do my bxst."

Sunday school class-s, commit--s, th- board, th- m-n's, wom-n's and childr-n's groups, and th- youth groups all hav- many m-mb-rs, so if I miss it won't b- notic-d, lik- the old typ-writ-r. But you ar- a k-y p-rson, and wh-n you don't do your b-st, nothing -ls- around you works out th- way it's suppos- d to.

So, if w- want -vrything to work out, all of our k-ys n--d to b- working, and -v-rything will work th- way it is suppos-d to.

It's lik- wh-n mom call-d us to supp-r. The tabl- just wasn't right until -v-ryon- was th-r-, just lik- wh-n you ar-n't th-r-.

Luke 11:52 *"Woe to you experts in the law, because you have taken away the key to knowledge. You yourselves have not entered, and you have hindered those who were entering."*

"Father, you are always unbroken and there for me. I will be there for You. AMEN"

NEXT

How many times must I be assured I am saved? If that's all there is to my faith, I haven't been listening very well, for if I, by God's grace, have been forgiven and assured of a place in Heaven, then surely there's some response needed.

In 4:11-12 of Paul's letter to the Ephesians he says:

"He gave some to be apostles, some to be prophets, some to be evangelists, and some to be pastors and teachers, to prepare God's people for works of service, so that the body of Christ may be built up."

James, says in 2:24-26 *"You see that a person is justified by what he does and not by faith alone. As the body without the spirit is dead, so faith without deeds is dead."*

When I was a boy, playing ball, we would run toward the goal with a hand held high yelling, "I'm open, I'm open," letting the person with the ball know that we were ready for a pass. Shouldn't Christians be open and ready to serve?

I went to register our church van. A long line snaked back and forth, around and down the back hall. The word everyone in line was waiting to hear was "Next." When one of the clerks was open, she would call out, "Next," to let the first person in line know she was ready to help them.

Maria Schwarzenegger, wife of California's governor, had been on several TV shows talking about her new book, "One More Word Before You Go". She said she had visited her father, Sergeant Schriver, who asked, "What are you doing now." You see, he had raised his children to give back, to be servants and people helpers.

She said, "I just finished a book."

Then he said, "But it's finished. What are you doing now?"

God's call sounds like NEXT! Are you open? What are you doing now? He needs people for works of service.

"Father in Heaven, if you need me, I'm open." AMEN

I Forgot

I was ready to go to town, and went into the room where I keep my desk with my computer and files and all those things I deem important. When I change clothes or get ready for bed that is where I put my billfold and keys. I noticed how messy the desk was, and took a few minutes to straighten the top by putting some things in drawers, some things to do in a neat pile, and others in the trash can. I backed up and looked at it. "Very neat," I thought, and went out to get in the car. I reached in my pocket and realized I had no keys or billfold. I had gotten so involved in the straightening of my desk that I had forgotten what my mission was. It seems the older I get the more absent minded I become. Later, when I was looking at my Sunday school lesson, I looked up the word FORGET in my bible computer program. In the new Common English Bible (CEB) it appears 85 times. Some of its uses are good and some are, well, not so good. Here are seven of my favorites on forgetting.

From David's Psalms, *Let my whole being bless the* LORD *and never forget all his good deeds,* (Psalm 103:2). *I will delight in your statutes; I will not forget what you have said.* (Psalm 119:16).

Proverbs for living a good life. *My son, don't forget my instruction. Let your heart guard my commands.* (Proverbs 3:1) *Get wisdom; get understanding. Don't forget and don't turn away from my words.* (Proverbs 4:5)

[*Promises to Jacob and Jerusalem*] *Remember these things, Jacob; Israel, for you are my servant. I formed you; you are my servant! I won't forget you, Israel.* (Isaiah 44:21)

From Paul; *Brothers and sisters, I myself don't think I've reached it, but I do this one thing: I forget about the things behind me and reach out for the things ahead of me.* (Philippians 3:13)

Don't forget to do good and to share what you have because God is pleased with these kinds of sacrifices. (Hebrews 13:16)

Lord; *I won't forget, I promise.* AMEN

God Bless Our Founding Forefathers

The "Separation of Church and State," is found only in the first amendment to the constitution, also referred to as the "Bill of Rights. Look it up. **Amendment 1:** Freedom of religion, speech, and the press; rights of assembly and petition; _Congress shall make no law respecting an establishment of religion, or prohibiting the free exercise thereof;_ There isn't any more. What it says is that the government will not form any church or interfere with our churches or our worship. That's it.

On top of the Washington Monument are four plates. One is embossed: "Laus Deo." In English "Praise be to God!" On 12th Landing is a prayer offered by the City of Baltimore; on the 20th is a eulogy for George Washington presented by Chinese Christians from Ningo, Chekiang Province, China; on the 24th is a presentation made by Sunday School children from New York and Philadelphia quoting Proverbs 10:7, Luke 18:16 and Proverbs 22:6. Inside the cornerstone is a Holy Bible presented by the American Bible Society

These words to the governors of the 13 states are in <u>St. Paul's</u> chapel in New York City. _"Now I make it my earnest prayer that God would have you and the State over which you preside, in His holy protection, that He would incline the hearts of the citizens to cultivate a spirit of subordination and obedience to government, to entertain brotherly affection and love for one another, for their fellow citizens and the United States at large, and particularly for their brethren who have served in the field, and finally, that He would most graciously be pleased to dispose us all to do justice, to love mercy and to demean ourselves with that charity, humility and pacific temper of mind which were the characteristics of the Divine Author of our blessed religion and without an humble imitation of whose example in these things we can never hope to be a happy nation. I
have the honor to be, with much esteem and respect, Sir, your Excellency's most obedient and humble servant, George Washington."_

"Thank you Father for our founding fathers who believed in you and meant for our country to be a Christian nation. AMEN"

Christian Basics – Love and Good Works

In Matthew 22:37-40 *"37 Jesus replied:* *"'Love the Lord your God with all your heart and with all your soul and with all your mind.' 38 This is the first and greatest commandment. 39 And the second is like it: 'Love your neighbor as yourself. 40 All the Law and the Prophets hang on these two commandments."*

Matthew 25:35-36 *"35 For I was hungry and you gave me something to eat, I was thirsty and you gave me something to drink, I was a stranger and you invited me in, 36 I needed clothes and you clothed me, I was sick and you looked after me, I was in prison and you came to visit me."*

From Paul – I Corinthians 13:1-8, 13 *"1 If I speak in the tongues of men or of angels, but do not have love, I am only a resounding gong or a clanging cymbal. 2 If I have the gift of prophecy and can fathom all mysteries and all knowledge, and if I have a faith that can move mountains, but do not have love, I am nothing. 3 If I give all I possess to the poor and give over my body to hardship that I may boast, but do not have love, I gain nothing.*

4 Love is patient, love is kind. It does not envy, it does not boast, it is not proud. 5 It does not dishonor others, it is not self-seeking, it is not easily angered, it keeps no record of wrongs. 6 Love does not delight in evil but rejoices with the truth. 7 It always protects, always trusts, always hopes, always perseveres.

8 Love never fails. But where there are prophecies, they will cease; where there are tongues, they will be stilled; where there is knowledge, it will pass away.

13 And now these three remain: faith, hope and love. But the greatest of these is love."

"Lord, thank you for the gift of life, for your son, Jesus, and the joy we receive in loving you and serving others. AMEN"

End of Book One Devotionals

www.ingramcontent.com/pod-product-compliance
Lightning Source LLC
Chambersburg PA
CBHW061348140726
47997CB00003B/1109